CORPORATELY CHALLENGED

A Guide to Help Jump-Start Your Corporate Career

by JJ Lee

Copyright © 2018 by JJ Lee

All rights reserved. No part of this book may be reproduced in any manner without written permission except in the case of brief quotations included in critical articles and reviews. For information, please contact the author.

Cover Photograph from Rawpixel.com, modified by the author under the Creative Commons Zero (CC0) license.

Back Cover Photograph by Tirachard Kumtanom from Pexels.com used under the Creative Commons Zero (CC0) license.

First Edition First Printing

Contents

PREFACE: CORPORATELY CHALLENGED 1
   What Employers Want 2
   Who Am I? 3
   A Book I Never Expected to Write 4
   Not a Coming of Age Management Book 5

AGENDA ITEM 1: GREAT CORPORATE EXPECTATIONS 7
   There Is More Than One Corporate Ladder 7
   It's Easy to Be Average 8
   Money Talks 9
   Where is the Loyalty? 11
   Working for the Man(ager) 12
   Office Politics 12

AGENDA ITEM 2: THE MODEL OFFICE CITIZEN 15
   This is My Cube 16
   The Long-winded 18
   Decoding the Dress Code 18
   The Walking Sick 20
   The Germ Factory Known as the Computer Keyboard 21
   The Post-Lunch Battle 22
   Rocking the Music at Work 23
   The Unspoken Rules of Printing Etiquette 24
   What Your Breakroom Manners Reveal About You 26
   Seize the Lunch Hour! 28
   Working from Home or "Working from Home?" 29
   Overcome the Monday and Back from Vacation Blues 30
   Are Emojis Ok in Business Communications? 32
   Lipstick on a Pig Is Still a Pig! 33
   FROM THE CUBE FARM 34

AGENDA ITEM 3: I HAVE TO WORK WITH PEOPLE? 37
   "I Have Underwear Older Than You" 37
   High Five for Teamwork! 38
   The People You Work with Are Not Perfect, You Included 40

Finding Common Ground 42
The Gatekeepers of the Office 43
The Power of a Simple Hello 44
Have You Tried Turning It Off and On Again? 44
Departing Co-workers 46
Seeing Things Eye to Eye 46
Transition of Work 47
What's in a Name? Everything 48
Use the Employee Directory to Your Advantage 48
FROM THE CUBE FARM 49

AGENDA ITEM 4: BE SELFISH ABOUT YOUR CAREER 51

Is the Company a Good Fit for You? 52
You Are Not Your Worst Enemy 54
Be Prepared to Pay Your Dues 55
Status Reports 56
Getting Too Attached to Your Work 57
Be Proactive About Receiving Feedback 58
Finding Your Management Style 59
The High Potential Employee 59
The Continued Pursuit of Knowledge 62
Making Mistakes is Ok...As Long as It's Not a Big One 64
Office Street Cred 65
Setting Goals, a Necessary Evil 67
The Thing About Job Titles 69
Keep the Résumé Updated 70
Job Hunting, No One Has to Know 71
Stuff Happens, Be Prepared 72
Employee Perks 73
Start Building That Nest Egg as Early as Possible 73
Managing Your Manager 76
FROM THE CUBE FARM 78

AGENDA ITEM 5: PLEASING THE MEETING GODS 81

Chance Favors the Prepared Mind 81
It's Meeting Time 85
The Writing on the Whiteboard 87
Surviving Meetings 88

Rescheduling Meetings 89
International Meetings 90
FROM THE CUBE FARM 90

AGENDA ITEM 6: A PRESENTATION PRIMER 93
Getting into a Presentation Frame of Mind 94
Practice: Lather, Rinse, and Repeat 95
The Final Countdown 99
Other Presentation Considerations 101
Slideshows 102
FROM THE CUBE FARM 105

AGENDA ITEM 7: ERASING THE BROWSER HISTORY WON'T DO YOU ANY GOOD 109
Me, Myself, and My Selfies 109
Email Expectations 114
FROM THE CUBE FARM 119

AGENDA ITEM 8: BEHAVIOR BEYOND OFFICE BORDERS ... 121
After Work Party Time 121
Business Nom Noms 124
FROM THE CUBE FARM 127

AGENDA ITEM 9: A BUSINESS TRAVEL PRIMER 129
Travel Basics 129
Packing Considerations 132
FROM THE CUBE FARM 136

AGENDA ITEM 10: IN SEARCH OF GREENER PASTURES 139
Changing Employers? Things to Know Before You Go 139
You Have No Power Here! 143
FROM THE CUBE FARM 145

PARTING NOTES 149

ACKNOWLEDGEMENTS 151

PREFACE: CORPORATELY CHALLENGED

Corporately Challenged: Lacking fundamental office skills and understanding of corporate culture. Affected individuals can often be seen wasting other people's time at meetings, speaking off the slides during presentations, being passed on for promotions, and ordering everything on the menu at business dinners.

If you consider yourself to be corporately challenged, or want to develop your office acumen further, then this book is here to help. The objective of this book is to bring things that you would never consider to the forefront of your office skills radar, with the goal of educating you on developing essential soft skills and office know-how.

I wrote this book because there was nothing like it on the market when I first stepped foot into a corporate environment. I was corporately challenged, as green as they came. It took me years to learn the ropes to become a strong corporate citizen. Many realizations and lessons learned came from mistakes made on the job, through observation of others, and advice shared by mentors and executives. Since I can't go back in time and share this information with my younger self, I can do the next best thing, to share it with you, with the intention of giving you the jump-start that I never had.

When you entered the corporate world for the first time, you probably realized that the courses you took in college didn't cover topics on how to navigate the everyday nuances and situations faced in the office. Along with business school students, graduates with STEM

(Science, Technology, Engineering, and Math), liberal arts, and other degrees usually end up working in white-collared positions. Wouldn't it be neat if higher education institutions offered a course that teaches basic office skills knowledge and how corporations function? It would hold much value for those who have decided to spend a significant portion of their lives in an open box under lousy fluorescent lighting. Talk about a wasted opportunity. It could be an elective made available to all students, regardless of the major they choose. If you have yet to step foot in a corporate environment, you're in for a surprise. Textbook and classroom education make up only a small percentage of the knowledge gained over your lifetime, you've only scratched the surface.

What Employers Want

There is no guaranteed formula for career success, but there are two types of skills that employers expect from their employees, strong hard and soft skills. Hard skills are the academic and job-specific elements that you bring to the position, basically, your expertise on the subject matter. For example, a financial analyst's hard skills would be conducting financial research through the use of specific software and finance formulas. A computer programmer's hard skills would be proficiency in understanding computer languages and the ability to write good code. Soft skills refer to the non-technical and human interaction elements. For example, career management, collaboration, leadership, problem-solving, communication, innovation, and time management. Employers highly covet both types of skills, but unfortunately, not all employees exhibit those traits. For the most part, a thorough interview process will most likely result in selecting a strong candidate. However, interviews lack visibility when it comes to assessing meeting skills, office etiquette knowledge, career management skills, and common sense. The interviewers may have a good idea of where the candidate stands, but it can be a hit or miss.

While having competent hard and soft skills are pivotal, when pairing them with office know-how (a specific set of skills that help us navigate through daily office life and a topic that this book will cover), the combination of the three types of skills will form the office knowledge threesome...does that sound weird? How about the office knowledge trinity? Maybe the tri-force of office knowledge?

Who Am I?

I grew up in the family restaurant business, doing almost every task my parents could throw at me. It was their career, not mine. Sick of the dirty dishwater that would leach into dishwashing gloves that never seemed to be long enough for the deep sinks and the deep fryer oil splatter that was near impossible to avoid, I applied to business school. There was no way I was going to inherit the restaurant, and I'm pretty sure my parents sent me to college so I wouldn't. A majority of my career was spent working in companies ranked in the Fortune 500 and 100 lists. I'm one of those people who prefers to change jobs after several years, not because I get bored, but because I believe it's essential to work in different industries and companies as much as possible in order gain new experiences and perspectives. Say what you will, but company loyalty doesn't exist. As a former mentor once told me, "a rolling stone gathers no moss." My goal at each company was to learn as much as I could before looking for new challenges elsewhere. Doing so led me on eye-opening business trips across the world.

I started my career as an analyst at a large global banking firm that employed hundreds of thousands of employees. At the time of writing this book, I believe it is the second largest bank in the world in terms of market capitalization. That means I was just a number in the system, one of many worker bees gathering precious honey for their corporate overlords. It was as entry-level as it got. The pay was crap, and I lost count the number accidents I've narrowly avoided while making the daily 120-mile round trip commute by car. You probably won't believe the number of mistakes I've made the first year on the job, but my manager told me it was ok to make mistakes as long as I didn't repeat them. That advice may have worked on my younger self, but today I have a different perspective on that.

A year later, I left for an opportunity at another global bank where I quickly rose through the ranks leading cross-functional teams and managing projects. Recognized by management as a high potential employee, it led to promotions, placing me in a more senior position than some teammates who were twice my age. I'm pretty sure they didn't like being outranked by someone who still looked like he was fresh out of kindergarten. High potentials are employees that companies invest and develop into leaders. That means more training opportunities, leadership career paths, and better visibility.

The company took a financial hit from the 2008 subprime mortgage crisis, and I accepted a team leadership position at a pharmaceutical company. Unfortunately, I fell hard off the corporate ladder due to an acquisition. The layoff, a blessing in disguise, led me to the transportation industry. There I worked with middle and upper-level management on implementing information technology processes at the corporate level. There too, I was recognized as a high potential employee and was promoted to a team lead. Eventually, I longed for a position that would give me the autonomy to do things my way. I was ready to be the boss. By that time, I was ready to put my recently obtained Master's degree to use.

I left behind companies that identified employees by a number to a much smaller one where everyone seemed to know my name. In my current position at a medium-sized firm, I get to be the big fish in my pond. Not only do I work with middle and upper management, but also the C-Suite (CEO, CIO, COO, etc.), with a high level of independence. Even though I am still working for "the man," for the first time, I feel that this is the right place for me. How long will I stay? Only time will tell, but in the meantime, I'm going to learn as much as I can and take advantage of any career-enhancing opportunity that comes my way.

A Book I Never Expected to Write

There was never any intention to write a book about office life. The book I envisioned writing was one of epic sci-fi and fantasy. It would be a story of the hero saving the damsel in distress while kicking a space monster in its extraterrestrial gonads. This book is not it, far from it. The writing started out as a joke, but at some point, I found writing about office life quite therapeutic.

The idea for office life writing came to me on a Friday night some time ago. A few friends and I were in the car driving around the city in search of a bar to begin an evening of relaxation and drinks, which meant, we would drink until our bodies relaxed or passed out. The conversation in the car transitioned from silly banter to talking about our jobs. Seriously, who the heck killed the mood? It turned out that they were all going through the same struggles and hardships in dealing with office politics and doing their best to succeed. No one was happy with their jobs. They were bored, unchallenged, and tired of business traveling. There I was, in a car with a bunch of adults in their late twenties stuck on the corporate ladder and sick of their jobs, no wonder they needed a drink.

Not a Coming of Age Management Book

Corporately Challenged is not one of those "how to be a manager" books. Reading those types of books seeking an answer on how to be a manager may turn you into a management chimera that's destined to fail. You know what's going to help you become a manager? By building a strong foundation of office skills, understanding the corporate game, and understanding that climbing the ladder may not be a straight shot to the top. You'll figure it out over time. Eventually, a profound moment of clarity will indicate that you're ready to lead and manage others. Just call it a feeling.

The information in this book is written in an easy to digest format so that it may serve as a reference guide. Think of it as your office mentor. Embedded at the end of most agendas are sections called *From the Cube Farm* that contain real-life stories based on my office experiences.

There is no expectation for you to follow the guide down to every detail, but read on and see what may benefit you. Don't worry. The book won't judge you like some of your co-workers.

AGENDA ITEM 1: GREAT CORPORATE EXPECTATIONS

If you're planning to invest in a corporate career, or are already doing so, you will or probably already have realized that corporate life isn't filled with rainbows and unicorns. It's more like a dog rolling in its feces, and then jumping on the brand new white couch. Well, it's not that bad, but there's no yellow brick road for you to follow, in fact, the corporate landscape can be unpredictable, disenchanting, and downright hostile. It will chew you up and spit you out if you're not careful. I bet the textbooks you read in school never told you about that.

When working for the man, there are many things not under your control, but the information in this book will help you to make the best of it. I entered my first corporate job bright-eyed and bushy-tailed, and after working for so many years, my tail isn't as bushy as it used to be, and some grey hairs may be randomly popping up, but there's still a twinkle in my eyes because I do enjoy working in a corporate environment. Before we get down to the details, it's important to understand how the corporate world functions at its basic level.

There Is More Than One Corporate Ladder

First, let's talk about the corporate ladder. Sure, you know what that is. It's the imaginary climbing apparatus that leads to prestigious job titles and rank. We all dream of it, to rise from the position of a low-level employee, into the gates of management, and eventually, the top, a place reserved for the elite. Well, it didn't take long for me to realize that climbing the corporate ladder was much more difficult than imagined. There are many barriers to overcome.

Each company has its corporate ladder, meaning each one is unique. It may be easy to move up the ladder at one company, and be extremely difficult at another. The reason is due to differences in corporate culture, performance management processes, organizational structure, company size, corporate political environment, and competition with other people who are hungry to move up the ladder as well. There are office sycophants who will try to kick you off the ladder, making sure you land face first. Remember, as you take a step on each rung of the ladder, you're climbing at your own risk. Corporate ladders don't come with warning labels, and there is a chance you may slip, or fall off entirely.

When I first started working for a large corporation, my objective was to climb the corporate ladder as quickly as possible. I was more concerned with chasing titles and handing out business cards than building a solid foundation (I have the business card scene in the movie *American Psycho* to blame for that). I'm sure many others out there share the same sentiment. While I was learning critical skills on how to perform on the job, there wasn't any guidance on which skills would help my career growth, the skills that would increase the chances of stepping up to the next rung. I had to rely on myself.

It's Easy to Be Average

It's not difficult to obtain an average employee rating during annual performance reviews. As long as you do the job and don't mess up, you're good. Being average may award you with modest raises, bonuses, and eventually a promotion. Are you ok being left behind by high potential employees who are hell bent in seeking leadership development opportunities, increased organizational visibility, and a better career path within the company? If you're not ok with that, are you willing to do more than what's expected of you? If being considered average is good enough, realize that you may be forfeiting better and more fulfilling job opportunities. Being average may end up working against you if you lose your job. Ask yourself right now, how well do you think you stack up with other people in the job market who have the same job function and skills as you? If you were to compete with them for a job, who do you think would emerge as the stronger candidate, or maybe perhaps as THE candidate?

Money Talks

Talking about money is important. If money is the primary driver of how you selected your career path, that's ok, as long as you're competent in what you do. After all, that's why you went to school right? To enter the real world with prospects of financial independence and moving out of mom's basement so you can do whatever the heck you want. The path to big money is not quick and easy unless you come across a windfall of cash, marry rich, or successfully heist diamonds and manage to fence them. Someone told me in the past that you're never going to get rich working for the man, but let's face it, you can. It depends on how hard you work, how you manage finances, how much potential others see in you, and not only seizing opportunities, but also excelling at them. Naturally, some job junctions pay more than others, and that can vary depending on location. A $100,000 salary is going to go much further in a city in Texas than San Francisco. For most of us, it will take time to accumulate wealth and status. Since company performance affects annual raises, they are not guaranteed. My biggest pay raises came when I changed employers and negotiated the starting salary. It's important to negotiate the salary, even if the company comes back with a small increase over the original offer amount. Most companies average between 2-3% for annual raises, which may not seem like much, but if you can negotiate a higher starting salary, you will benefit in the long term. Take a look at the following example and table.

The employer offers a salary of $50,000. You accept without negotiating. Let's see how much you make if you work for the company for five years, not including tax and other deductions, assuming a 3% annual pay increase. Now, what if you managed to negotiate a higher starting salary? Say an additional $3,000. It may not seem like much at first, but in the following table, the numbers show that you'll be better off, especially in the long run.

Earnings After 5 Years at 3% Annual Pay Increase

Years	Taking Salary as Offered	Negotiating a Higher Salary (ex. $3,000 more)
Year 1	$ 50,000	$ 53,000
Year 2	$ 51,500	$ 54,590
Year 3	$ 53,045	$ 56,228
Year 4	$ 54,636	$ 57,915
Year 5	$ 56,275	$ 59,652
Total	$ 265,457	$ 281,384

Just by asking if the employer could do a little better regarding the salary, you have accumulated an extra $15,927 (ignoring deductions) over the years. Chump change or not, it's still extra money. I'm not advocating you to change jobs frequently because that can send red flags to potential employers, but sometimes, to move up in rank and salary, it's a better alternative than waiting to see what the company has in store for you come performance appraisal time.

Salary alone shouldn't be the ultimate factor in accepting a job offer. Think about job growth potential as well. Back in the day, my classmates boasted at how much their starting salaries were, and they picked the company with the highest salary offer. The fact that they received multiple job offers pissed me off. I remember one classmate was bragging about a signing bonus. I found out later that the company let him go because he had trouble fitting in and that the company wasn't for him.

Look for opportunities that will give you the skills and opportunities to grow over time, especially ones that empower you to make decisions. I changed employers one time for a modest salary increase, and people said I was crazy for accepting the offer. The company I moved to utilized a particular piece of software that many other companies were listing as a requirement on job postings. I thought about my future growth and made a move so that I could learn the particular piece of software in hopes that it would pay off in the future. On one occasion, I accepted a job position at a lower salary than the previous one. The opportunity was too good to pass up, and it worked out in the long run. In your career, you may not work exclusively for one company. That means you'll have to make decisions and take risks. Remember, there are many corporate ladders, and some are easier to climb than others. Moving across the scaffold to another ladder is considered career growth, even if there's no upward movement. As long as you keep learning new skills, you will grow. Sometimes you may have to make a lateral move before moving up.

Where is the Loyalty?

The idea of working for one company for life doesn't exist anymore. You're not expected to enter into a monogamous relationship with the employer. In fact, you should probably sleep around to find what works for you. Job security is also a thing of the past, don't let anyone fool you that you're not expendable. You are, we all are. I know many people who were unexpectedly laid off after giving decades of their lives to a company. Remember, companies can let employers go without cause and employees can leave their employer at will. I learned of an employee who suddenly stopped showing up to work after a couple of months. Eventually, the company found out the person was doing fine, but it was odd not to receive communication from the employee that he decided not to return to work. On another occasion, an employee quit after one day. It goes to show you that it's a dog eat dog world. There is no loyalty from either side.

From the board of directors' point of view, it's a numbers game. If the company is going through hard times, the option of laying off employees is always on the table because it's a practical cost-savings strategy. Layoffs are not personal, it's business, although it can feel like the company royally screwed you over. Sometimes it's important to change employers or industries since working for one company may limit your exposure to new opportunities and challenges. If there is something out there on the job market that interests you or will help your career growth, explore it. Nowadays, you're expected to. Loyalty is overrated.

Working for the Man(ager)

Usually, when I ask people if they love their job, the response is usually, "Meh, it's a job, it pays the bills." Or if I ask them how their day is, the response is usually SSDD (Same Shit, Different Day). And there are those who love their job. You're probably wondering, "What the heck are they smoking? Can I get some?" I'm a firm believer that job success and happiness correlates with how well the relationship is with the employee and the manager. Let's face it, the bigger the company, the more competition there is, and the less visibility. Finding the right job is just as important as finding the right manager. When it comes down to it, you're essentially working for the manager, not the company. With that said, it's important to know how you prefer to be managed compared to how your manager prefers to manage others. For example, if you're big on autonomy and don't like the feeling of someone constantly looking over your shoulder, then working for a micro-manager is going to make your life hell. A good manager will have your best interests in mind, challenge you, and provide opportunities for career growth.

Office Politics

The workplace is full of egos and political cow dung. You don't have to be strong-willed and hungry for success to work in corporate, but if you want to do well, you better know how to play the field and understand that office politics is something that is difficult to avoid. If you're not aware of any office politics that's going around, it may be because you haven't climbed the corporate ladder high enough to notice yet. However, there is something known as trickle-down politics. For example, you may be overlooked for a promotion simply because someone on the promotion review board doesn't like your manager on a personal level. By the way, that promotion that's supposed to be yours? Well, someone else in another department got it. Does that sound messed up? It does. There will be people who will try to manipulate you or others to gain an advantage, have you choose sides, or make "handshake" agreements behind others' backs. Office politics is the invisible hand that gets its grubby fingers into everyone's cookie jar and it's important for you to recognize it for what it is in your organization.

As you can see, corporate life isn't just about racing to the top and sharing business cards. However, that doesn't mean you can't make the best of it. Unfortunately, as hard as you need to work to perform the task at hand, you also have to work hard to manage your career, and a significant portion of that is going to be proving to your employer that your are a worthy investment. Look, I'm sure you already have the hard skills required for the job, what's going to help set you apart is your soft skills and office know-how.

AGENDA ITEM 2: THE MODEL OFFICE CITIZEN

In the typical American education system, a college student will have completed about 17 years of formal classroom education upon graduation. However, the transition from the classroom to the office isn't seamless. The kiddie pool floaties are abruptly ripped off, and the new graduates are tossed into the deep end to fend for themselves. It's a heck of a welcome into the real world, and there won't be any hand holding. It's sink or swim. To think about it in the grand scheme of things, the 17 years spent in the classroom are nothing compared to the next 45 or so years in the office, or until a robot takes over your job and kicks you to the curb, but that's a discussion for another time.

According to the National Center for Education Statistics: The Condition of Education 2017, of the 1,920,718 bachelor degrees awarded by postsecondary institutions for the 2015-2016 academic year, 371,694 were business degrees[1]. That's approximately 19% of all awarded degrees. Keep in mind, a large number of graduates with computer science, engineering, science, liberal arts, and other degrees are probably working in an office environment as well. How many of those graduates do you think would have benefited from an office skills development class? Many people who are already working could also benefit from such a class.

Navigating the cube farms is no easy task. Each company's culture has its set of values and norms. What may apply at one company may not apply at another, yet, human behavior across different businesses and industries remains pretty much the same. How many times have you said, "Oh boy, I have dealt with this type of person!" before?

That's the stuff that makes office life so intriguing. You get to work with people of different personalities and cultures. Sometimes it feels like office life is just a game and we are on the board aiming for a particular prize. Some want to make it to the top with a prestigious title, and others wish to make a lot of money. There are those who want to do the bare minimum amount of work to stay in the game, and of course, some are still figuring out the rules. At some point in your career, you will know which types of people will help your career grow and which will hold you back. You may be holding yourself back and not even realize it.

Office know-how is a type of management skill used to handle day-to-day office affairs. For example, if you drink the last of the coffee, you should brew a new pot, or if you're sick, you need to stay home. Much of it comes down to the unspoken rules of the office and using common sense, but guess what? Common sense isn't common. Developing office know-how skills is as important as developing hard skills and soft skills. If you're "that guy" who is inconsiderate of others and presents poor office etiquette, people will perceive you negatively. If your negative reputation precedes you, then it's going to be an uphill battle.

This is My Cube

Repeat after me, "This is my cube. There are many others like it, but this one is mine." Cubicles of various shapes, configurations, and sizes dominate the office floor. Some are rather plain, some partially decorated, and some look like the person permanently moved in. Personally, I think, it's not a good idea to over-personalize or decorate the cube since it doesn't present a professional image. I know a handful of people who took decorating inspiration from a local roadhouse restaurant and it isn't pretty.

Years ago, I met with my manager, who was an executive director, and noticed his office was void of decorations and personal effects. I mentioned his office was kind of barren. In turn, he replied: "It's because if the company ever lets me go, I can just pack my bags and leave on the spot." While his point of view was a bit pessimistic, he explained that it makes it easier to sever ties with the company and that personalizing his workspace might form strong emotional bonds with the company. In essence, he didn't want to create a home away from home and preferred a clean breakup. He had been with the company for a while and said that he was not immune from being let go (no one is). About a year and a half after I left the company, a former colleague told me that the company laid him off. Talk about self-fulfilling prophecies.

I took his advice and continued to adopt it after I changed employers. It so happened that I was laid off due to a company acquisition. After receiving the news about the severance package, I returned to my drab cubicle, picked up my messenger bag, and left. It was a clean break. At certain companies, people who were just laid off are not allowed to pack their personal effects and are led straight out the front door by a security escort. What's the reason for immediate dismissal and not giving someone time to pack and leave? Companies are afraid that employees may try to sabotage business assets before they depart, or even worse, return and spray bullets everywhere (scary but true). Usually, someone will pack your personal effects, and the company will mail them to the address on file. Sometimes it's hard to walk by overdecorated cubicles of people who have been recently laid off. It's as if the cubicle is telling the person's life story. While it took me one day to move from my apartment to my house, it took my coworker two days to move his items out of the cubicle after being laid off.

If there is another reason for you not to go ape-crazy with cubicle personalization, it's that there may be kleptomaniacs in the office. Don't bring anything expensive, sentimental, or irreplaceable to work. They may disappear. There is also a risk of having your personal effects damaged if there happens to be a fire or water leak at the office. It's better to leave such things at home. I remember the time when a major storm caused the building sewage drains to spew out of the toilets. The unpleasantness made its way down to the floors below. Imagine being at your desk and all of a sudden, it starts raining over your workspace. I'm willing to bet no one expected a forecast of indoor showers with a chance of poop. A biohazard team was called in to quarantine a section of the building, and many people's personal effects were either packed up for decontamination or trashed.

The Long-winded

Many social butterflies would rather spend their days talking with others than doing work. These people love to talk about themselves. They tend to blab excessively with no end in sight. A brief conversation can quickly turn into the state of the union address. The problem is that you have already tuned them out after the first minute and the only words coming out of your mouth are: "uh-huh," "yeah," or "that's nice." You need to end the conversation and resist the urge to tell the person to shut up. As you start to back away, the person is still talking, not knowing when to take a hint.

Usually, it's easier to interrupt the person and explain that you have to go and that you want to continue the conversation some other time. However, you're not obligated to continue the conservation later. Now, you may be thinking to yourself, "Why do people like to talk so much?" It's probably because the office environment may be the only place where they can have conversations with others.

However, too much talking can get on other people's nerves, especially if they always end up being one-sided. If you're thinking to yourself, "Wow, I have never encountered a co-worker who just blabs on and on." You may be the person who yaps too much.

Engaging in a bit of personal conversation with co-workers is fine as long as it's not offensive or distracting people from their work. If your voice travels, think about people in the adjacent area. Some are bound to eavesdrop, and some will become agitated. If all you do is chat with others around the office all day, people will notice and wonder if you're even there to work.

Decoding the Dress Code

Personal grooming and dress reflect who you are, and people notice what you wear. Dress like a slob and people will perceive you as a slob. Dress nice, and people will think you are well put together, even if you're not. Someone once told me to dress for the job I want, not for the job I have. That is bad advice. No, that is horrible advice. Just because you want to be a superhero, it doesn't mean you should show up to work dressed like Batman or Wonder Woman, maybe unless it's Halloween. The best way to dress for work is to follow the company dress code policy and use common sense. It's better to dress up a bit than down. For some reason, many people think the dress code is up to interpretation.

Business Professional. Most corporations adopt a business casual dress code, but if you work at a place that requires formal business attire, look for something that can add a tad of individualism, such as a nice pair of shoes, or light jewelry. Custom fit clothing is also a great way to go.

Business Casual. There are still varying levels of what business casual constitutes. Usually, there are summer business casual guidelines, and those to follow for the rest of the year. Refer to the company's dress code when in doubt. An ex-manager used to give me flack for wearing jeans around the office. That was until I threw the dress code policy in his face. Days later, he started wearing jeans.

Casual/Casual Fridays. This dress code doesn't mean to arrive at work in sweatpants and a hoodie or your lazy Sunday outfit. You still need to look presentable, groomed, and neat. I once wore a hoodie to work and got into a bit of trouble since the attire was deemed too casual. A coworker was about to report me to human resources, but the administrative assistant stopped him and gave me a heads up. It pays to be on the good side of administrative assistants.

Business Trip Dress Codes. Find out what the dress code is when you travel on business. If you're meeting a client or conducting business at another company, ask your contact what people there typically wear. You don't want to show up wearing business casual when everyone else is wearing business professional.

General Tips
- Wear clothes that fit well. Loose-fitting garments look sloppy and tight ones may reveal what's more than necessary, like inappropriate bulging.
- Take the time to groom. Enough said.

- Guys, clip your fingernails.
- Shower and practice good dental hygiene. You may not be able to smell your own stench, but others will. Body odor and bad breath is a natural human deterrent.
- Avoid revealing too much skin, cleavage, chest hair, etc.
- Iron your clothes or wear wrinkle-free clothes. It's not flattering if you look like a crumpled piece of paper.
- If jeans are allowed, choose dark denim over light colored denim. Make sure there are no holes or tattered bottoms.
- Clean and polish your shoes regularly. People notice the shoes!
- Keep flashy colors to a minimum. People will wonder why there is a hi-lighter marker walking around the office.
- Wear a dressy timepiece. Sure, you have a smartphone that tells the time, but a lovely watch can complete an outfit.
- There is no need to spend excessive amounts of money on designer brand name clothes, people in the office are most likely not going to ask to see the designer tag. Just look neat and professional.
- If you wear cologne or perfume, be aware of the amount you wear. There is a difference between smelling good and committing olfactory harassment. You may have become desensitized to the fragrance over time and may spray on more than what's necessary. People who are extremely sensitive to cologne and perfume may purposely avoid those who wear too much of it.

The Walking Sick

We people are an odd species. When we're not sick, we call (or email) out to play hooky, but when we are sick, we bring it to the office. We've all been there. That spot in the back of the throat starts to itch. We play it off as nothing, only to become a walking plague by lunch hour. "Nah, as long as I stay away from people it should be ok," you rationalize to yourself. Two hours later, you're hacking, coughing, and oozing body fluids from every orifice, thinking that co-workers don't notice. They do. Keep those germs away from the office. Besides, the feeling of knowing that you infected your co-workers is quite horrible.

I know, I know, you have too much work to do, and you cannot afford to take a day off. Why not ask to see if you can work from home for the day? You won't lose much productivity if you have the right tools available, and you will be doing everyone a favor by not spreading germs. If working from home isn't an option, take the day off.

On occasion, you do become sick. Not "sick" but actually sick. The standard operating procedure is to call or email the company or the manager and give notice. Well, if you're still functional, don't get back to bed after giving notice because you are obligated to inform others as well. If possible, cancel meetings you have scheduled for that day and inform the invitees. If you are not able to do so, see if someone in the office can do it for you, like a colleague or the manager. It's bad practice to take a sick day knowing there will be people in the meeting room waiting for you to show up. Setting up an out of office message is also a nice touch.

Similar to how children get sick from interacting with one another and sharing toys, it's quite easy to catch someone else's bug at the office. Everyday actions, such as shaking hands, pressing elevator buttons, and touching other common area items may place you at risk. One of the most straightforward methods to prevent infection is to wash your hands regularly or use hand sanitizer. Consider the office as a giant germ-infested playground. Don't believe me? Go to the break room's microwave and notice the fingerprint smudges on the door release button.

The Germ Factory Known as the Computer Keyboard

If you were offered five dollars to lick a keyboard that's sitting on a random desk in the office, would you? I'm not talking about a light dab of the tongue on the space bar, but one where you have to depress each letter or number from the beginning of one row of keys to the end. Is five dollars not enough? So, what's your price? Picture the colonies of microorganisms that are having orgies between the keys, laced with food bits, finger dandruff, nose goblins, rogue hairs, and other questionables.

Computer keyboards are perhaps the most frequently touched piece of equipment in the office and seldom cleaned. Ask yourself, when was the last time you cleaned the keyboard by shaking it upside down until all the small bits of nastiness fall out and meticulously wiping down each key and every crevice? If you're still trying to figure it out, then it's been way too long.

You eat, you touch the keyboard. You sneeze, you touch the keyboard. You shake hands with someone, and then you touch the keyboard. You go to the bathroom and forget to wash your hands (let's hope not), you touch the keyboard. You let someone else touch your keyboard because you need help with a spreadsheet formula (did they wash their hands after going to the bathroom?). I think it eventually dawned on computer manufacturers that producing off-white colored keyboards was not the best idea. The keys eventually take on a dark yellow hue from filthy finger contact and guess what, it is almost impossible to remove. A British research study was onducted some years back to see how dirty the typical office keyboards can be. It turns out they harbored more bacteria than the office's toilet seats. That's right, the toilet seats that have graciously supported many butts throughout the day are cleaner. Maybe it's because they undergo more frequent cleaning than keyboards do. At the very least, turn the keyboard over the wastebasket to shake out debris and wipe it down at least once a week. Compressed air is great for blowing out remaining debris. The individually packaged alcohol wipes from local drug stores or disinfecting wipes are a practical way to keep the keyboard sanitary. Chicklet style keyboards are popular with laptops such as Macbooks. They are typically easier to maintain since there are fewer crevices for debris to fall into. However, liquid spills may be tough to clean. I'm no stranger to destroying keyboards, the worst spills have got to be oatmeal and milk. If the keyboard is beyond cleaning, have it replaced. The IT department should have plenty in stock.

The Post-Lunch Battle

You return to work after eating a delicious lunch. The food has provided much nourishment and sustenance. Productivity is increasing, and there is nothing to stop you from meeting that deadline. Suddenly, your old friend Food Coma, decides to pay a visit. And guess what? It doesn't look like a happy camper. It lunges at you with a devastating left hook! You manage to duck out of the way as there is no way you're going to be knocked out. It comes back strong with a straight punch to the face. Dazed, you manage to land a solid uppercut on its ugly chin. The match is a close one, but there can only be one winner. Not backing down, it readies its haymaker and lets loose. You put up your defenses, but it's no use, the punch lands flush! Desperate times call for drastic measures as you resort to cheap shots. The low blows, biting, and eye gouges are ineffective. It winds up for one last punch, and you know what's coming. As the light turns to darkness, you're in a food-coma induced nap. Let's hope no one catches you sleeping on the job.

The onset of food-coma is by no means easy to avoid. By the time it rears its ugly head, it may be too late to get away from its crosshairs. Typical symptoms include lethargy, heavy eyelids, drowsiness, and in some cases, periods of microsleep to passing out. However, if you happen to feel the slightest onset of fatigue, take action immediately. Get out of your chair and start moving. The longer you wait and try to fight it, the worse it will be. Go to the bathroom, the break room, take a short walk, or drink something caffeinated. The key is to keep active until the drowsiness wears off.

Rocking the Music at Work

These days, it seems to be acceptable in most office environments to listen to music with headphones as long as it doesn't disturb others. Many people listen to music to either help them focus or block out office chatter, maybe even a bit of both. There are a few things to keep in mind.

Volume Awareness. If you're drowning out external noise with music, chances are you're going to be oblivious to hearing the phone ring, when someone calls your name, or when someone sneaks up on you, like your boss. If people are trying to get your attention by throwing things at you, that's a bad sign. Also, make sure the music doesn't bleed out of the headphones, which may disturb your neighbors.

Downsize. Avoid wearing the big and bulbous hi-fidelity surround sound headphones. They look unprofessional. Instead, invest in a set of quality earbuds or less conspicuous headphones that don't scream "I'm a DJ."

Consider Earplugs. If all you care about is drowning out background noise, simple foam earplugs should do the trick. Most convenience or hardware stores carry them.

Go Lo-Fi. Consider listening to a popular genre of music known as lo-fi hip-hop, as well as other variants such as chillhop and chillstep. These genres of music are great to have on while studying or at work. YouTube has many channels dedicated to these music genres, and the content creators work hard to keep the music fresh. A bit of a warning though, sometimes the music can be a bit too relaxing and cause drowsiness.

Background Noises. If music isn't your thing, there are plenty of websites that stream a variety of background sounds such as café chatter, nature sounds, and different types of noise, which are known to improve focus and concentration.

The Unspoken Rules of Printing Etiquette

There's no doubt that the multi-functional office printer still has its place in the office, even though many companies are trying to reduce their tree-killing footprint. While many businesses encourage employees to be mindful of the environment before printing, there's something about reading text off of a piece of paper that a computer monitor can't replicate. The use of office printers for occasional personal printing is an accepted norm. Don't take it for granted. Guess what happens when you print personal documents, and people are already at the printer waiting for theirs? Anything they pick up is fair game for viewing.

Don't Be a Printer Hog. The printer you use at work is most likely shared with others unless you're special and have your own. While the printer is spewing out copies of a hundred-page document, it's holding up twenty smaller print jobs in the queue. Guess what? Your print job is sitting pretty at number 20, and you need printouts for a meeting that starts in five minutes. The urge to cancel the large print job is looking extremely attractive, isn't it? But you're not a jerk and resist the temptation. It's best not to be a printer hog during prime business hours. If you ever have to print out many copies or a large document, it would be wise to split the printing into smaller jobs or schedule to do it when fewer people are around, such as towards the end of the day, lunch hour, or before the start of business day.

I Picked Up Your Copy by Accident. A fair amount of personal emails and other documents spew out of the shared office printers. Even though everyone occasionally prints out nonwork-related documents, the amount of information those people are willing to print out is unbelievable. What's even more obscene is that those personal documents are left sitting in the output tray for hours, even days. Let me set the record straight. I don't pick up other people's documents and read them for fun (most of the time). It's just that my print outs end up in the same output bin, and I inadvertently pick up documents that aren't mine. Occasionally, I do come across a few gems:
- Printouts of dating site matches and introductory emails.
- Printouts of personal pictures. Way to go, the yellow cartridge just got used up, and now the printer won't print even though all the other ink cartridges are full. May I recommend an online photo service instead? They come out much better.
- Printouts containing personal financial information, such as mortgage statements and job salary information. Dear co-worker, it may be time to refinance, and ask for a raise.

Low Toner? Shake It Like A Polaroid Picture. If your printed copy is faded and has streak marks, it may be time for toner replacement. Sometimes, giving the toner cartridge a few vigorous shakes may extend its life for a short while, but you can only shake it so many times until it needs replacement. If someone else is responsible for replacing it, let that person know. If you have access to the toner and know how to replace the cartridge, do it yourself. Don't walk away and let someone else do more shaking.

Refill the Paper Bin. If a large print job is necessary, make sure the printer has enough paper stocked. Many times, the print queue pauses because some person is printing a 200-page document when there are only 50 sheets of paper left in the tray, and has no idea the printer is out of paper.

Clear Paper Jams. There is always someone whose print job causes a paper jam, yet refuses to clear it. If your print job jams the printer, attempt to clear it or to call tech support for assistance.

What Your Breakroom Manners Reveal About You

The break room (aka pantry, canteen, coffee room, etc.) is a high traffic area during certain times of the day. It's usually busiest in the morning when everyone is settling in and looking to fuel up on caffeine, during lunch hour, and usually around the 3:00 PM mark. Unfortunately, it's also the place where you can learn a lot about your coworkers. Especially about the things they like to eat and whether or not they clean up after themselves. A coworker once told me, "If you think they are sloppy at the office, they are probably just the same or worse at home."

It's Easy to Spot the Slobs, Don't Be One of Them. The office is full of slobs. You know, those who spill drinks and don't bother to clean up the messes they make. Eyesores such as coffee splatter and food stains on tables and countertops are left on their own to dry and shrivel. It reveals a lot about that person, does it not? I wonder if they act the same way at home. Maybe there's someone who cleans up after them, and they expect the same at work. Just because there's a cleaning crew, it doesn't mean people should leave their messes for others to clean up. Do the right thing. I knew someone at a previous employer who always cleaned up other people's messes, and no, it wasn't the janitor. There are still good people left in this world.

Yes, Lunch Theft is Still a Thing. You have been waiting all morning for this moment, and damn it, you deserve it. It's lunchtime. You walk over to the refrigerator to retrieve the lunch you placed inside earlier. Well, it's no longer in the same position where you left it, no worries, someone may have moved it to make space. You search around the other shelves and side compartments, nothing. Your pulse intensifies. Not only can you feel it, but also hear it. The panic starts to set in. You have become a victim of a lunch theft. Even though your name is on the container, some jerkface still went ahead and stole it. And not only that, the culprit is enjoying it to the very last bite.

If the refrigerator is usually full of packed lunches, try to hide your's in the back of the lowest shelf behind other people's. At the very least, your food should not be in the front for easy pickings. What's that saying about outrunning a bear? You don't have to outrun the bear, just the slowest person. Another alternative would be to bring an insulated bag with a reusable cold pack and keep it at your desk.

Microwave Manners. The magical science oven has brought much joy into our lives, but many people fail to understand that it's a shared appliance. There are proper rules and etiquette to follow when it comes to using the work microwave. These rules also apply to toaster ovens.

- **Don't Heat up Stinky Food.** Either the heated food smells delicious, or it smells like something crawled inside and died. If a meal has the potential to funk up the office, be considerate of others and heat it up elsewhere with fewer people whenever possible. Regarding microwaveable popcorn, make sure to share it and not just the smells. Some companies ban microwave popcorn because it is considered an olfactory disturbance. If you ask me, microwaving cheese should be banned.
- **Don't Go MIA While Your Food Is Heating Up.** When heating up your food in the microwave for a couple of minutes, don't walk away and return 10 minutes later. Don't annoy hungry people. There may be others waiting to use it immediately after you. Some people may remove your lunch out of the microwave if you're not there for the final beep. If you don't want others touching your food, stick around.
- **Wipe down that Mess.** If you make a mess in the microwave, do the right thing, clean it up.
- **Reset the Timer.** If you take the food out before the beeps, remember to reset it for the next person.

Pre-rinse China and Glassware. If your employer provides china and glassware, then someone has to wash it or place it in a dishwasher. It's kind of messed up if you throw a plate of half-eaten mashed potatoes into the sink for someone else to scrape off. Clean your china and glassware as much a possible before placing it in the sink or dishwasher.

Seize the Lunch Hour!

It's lunchtime, so stop whatever you're working on, and step away from your desk. The lunch hour is yours. In fact, it's the only time during work where you're not expected to be productive by your employer, so take advantage of it. However, do you use up the entire lunch hour? According to the *2016-2017 State of Enterprise Work Report* by Workfront, 57% of general office workers get 30 minutes or less, with 28% taking 15 mins or less[2] for lunch.

Get Fit. The lunch hour is an opportunity to squeeze in a bit of physical fitness into the day. Many people take advantage of the time by going to the gym or taking a nice long walk around the vicinity of the office. It's an excellent way to break up the day, plus you will be doing something positive for your body. You may be surprised at how many people in your office go to the gym, and it's often a great place to meet new individuals in the company to expand your network. A mid-day workout session is a perfect remedy to break up the mundane workday. Since gym memberships can be expensive, especially in metropolitan areas, find out if the company subsidizes memberships at local gyms or if your insurance carrier offers gym membership discounts.

Try Not to Eat at Your Desk. You will be tempted to return to work soon after finishing eating. Instead, go out to eat with co-workers or in a common dining area. At the very least, get away from your workspace for a short while, even for a few minutes.

Run Errands. Cross off items on your errands to-do list. The sooner you get them out of the way, the less you will have to do when you get home.

Be Constructive. Do something constructive. Read a book, indulge in personal writing, play Sudoku, study something of interest, plan your next vacation, or plan the weekend.

Sneak in a Nap. Take a nap if you can find someplace quiet and isolated. Falling asleep in your cube during the day doesn't count.

Bond with Your Team and Coworkers. Go out for a team lunch! It can be once a week, once a month, or as often as your team likes. It's an excellent way to bond with teammates.

Working from Home or "Working from Home?"

No longer are employees bound to their desks at the office. If you have the opportunity to work from home either full-time or part-time, there are two things to keep in mind. First, make sure you know what type of employee you are. Do you thrive in an office environment and crave social interaction with others or are you more productive when working from the confines of your home? Second, do you have the discipline to do so? Working from home is not a one-size-fits-all solution.

Of course, working from home brings many benefits. The commute is extremely short, for parents with young children, there's no need to send them to daycare, the company may cover the Internet cost, and showering, grooming, and dressing up are determined on an as-needed basis. Perhaps the best part of it is, you can fart as much as you want from the home office. It's not unusual for interview candidates to ask about flexible work hours or work from home options.

If you're like me, then you prefer to be in the office. I feel more productive in the office. My reasons for preferring to work in the office are simple. I don't want to be stuck in the house all day, I like interacting with other people and learning from them to build relationships, and I want to be visible in the office by others. Otherwise, it's out of sight, out of mind. If you have trouble focusing when working from home, perhaps the following tips may help.

Minimize Distractions. If things such as electronics, housework, spouse, kids, pets, or basement goblins easily distract you in your home, working from home may not suit you. Find a quiet area to minimize disruptions.

Don't Be Tempted by the Bedroom. Avoid working in the bedroom because the bed can be inviting. You see, the bed is lonely and needs your warmth. It speaks in a sultry voice, "Hey there. It looks like someone is working hard. A little too hard if you ask me. Why don't you lie down on me while you work?" Nice try bed, nice try.

Develop a Routine. Do whatever you need to do before starting work and keep it consistent on the weekdays. It may be as simple as taking a morning poop and surfing the Internet, working out, making breakfast, or changing from sleepwear to a t-shirt and a pair of jeans, or going business casual. Maybe all of the above?

Of course, there are those who mess it up for the rest of us. Unfortunately, working from home is something that many people take for granted. It is a privilege, not a right. I knew co-workers who told me they were working from home, complete with hand quotations. One person at a company I used to work at was caught working for another company during his weekly work from home day. Because of these bad eggs, management is often apprehensive to permit employees to work from home. In 2013, Former Yahoo! CEO Marissa Mayer eliminated the work from home policy, explaining that employees are more productive when in the office. No doubt her decision drew a bit of criticism from the public, especially from those who are proponents of a flexible work style.

Overcome the Monday and Back from Vacation Blues

It's Monday morning, and you're wondering where the heck the weekend went. Face it, two days of rest is not enough. It was all a blur, and the Friday 5 o'clock whistle seems so out of reach. The best way to tackle the Monday blues is to set expectations right at the beginning of the week.

Collect Your Thoughts. The first impulse once arriving at your desk on Monday morning is to turn on the workstation and dig through emails. Fight that desire, and instead sit straight, close your eyes, take in a deep breath, and exhale. Clear your mind, keep taking deep breaths, keep those eyes closed, and visualize a mental map of the work you have to do for the week. Open your eyes and write down the week's tasks and goals on a notepad. The goal is to set the tone and expectations for the week that lies ahead, and the best way to do so is when your mind is calm, collected, and relaxed. It's not necessary to write anything in detail, just enough information to develop a roadmap to get started. Now you may turn on the computer and tackle those emails.

Prioritize. You have two choices here, to take care of the so-called low hanging fruit as a way to ease into the work week, or start on the more critical deliverables to jump start the week. It's the difference between slowly wading into the deep end of the pool or diving straight in. The choice is yours.

Pre-Vacation Prep. Perhaps one of the most stressful times to return to work is after a long and relaxing vacation. Well, to be honest, vacations may not be relaxing if you're always worrying about the work that's waiting for you back in the office. Picture this: yesterday you were on a beach with a tropical drink in hand, taking in the sunshine and the scent of the ocean. Today you're sitting in the cubicle with a computer mouse in hand and tolerating the funny smells coming from the adjacent cube. The notion of having to catch up on hundreds of emails and figuring where you left off is enough to question whether or not you took a long enough vacation. Maybe it was too soon to return. It's also a good idea to not leave things at the office hanging before you leave for vacation. You should consider:
- Setting an 'out of office' notice in your email program. If you have teammates who are covering for you during your absence, make a note of that. Mention if you will be checking email sporadically.
- Updating your voicemail message that you will be away.
- Writing a list of things that you have to do after returning from vacation. Setting expectations ahead of time will help to prevent a bit of stress and anxiety when you return from vacation and are scheduled to work the next business day.

- Notifying colleagues you work with before leaving for vacation. That way, if they need something from you, they will know to hold off.
- Finding someone to cover for you, if the workload is easily transferable.
- Taking the next day off after returning from vacation. Treat this as a day to reset before returning to work.

Are Emojis Ok in Business Communications?

The prevalence of instant messaging, texting, and social media has taken away the personal touch when it comes to people interaction. A side effect of electronic communications is that people are using shorthand, acronyms, poor grammar, and emojis to communicate. Emojis are so popular that they even have their own movie. Aspiring screenwriters are probably lighting their life-long screenplays on fire and throwing them in a metal trashcan. Using emojis when communicating on personal devices with friends and family is fine and all, but when those communication mannerisms are brought over to business communications, not only is it unprofessional but also those you're communicating with may think less of you. Business writing skills are more important than ever, and when someone uses an emoji in an email, our civilization dies a bit more each day.

Even if you're not much of a writer, find an outlet to write. Even better, see if you can take a business writing class. There will be a time when you will no longer only communicate with peers, but with upper management and even members of executive management. My line of work requires me to email communications to C-Level executives and when it comes to pressing that "send email" button, I double, even sometimes, triple check to make sure my message is on point. There is no place for emojis in business writing. I don't know if any of them would appreciate something like: Guess what? We missed the forecast numbers! Too Bad! :'(

A great method to learn how to write business emails is to observe firm-wide emails sent by executives or the marketing department. Chances are, those communications are held to a certain standard and members of the corporate communications department reviewed the content. What was it about those emails that made them so impactful? Was it the eloquence, delivery, clarity, or structure? Maybe a combination of those or all of the above? Are there things in those emails that you can adopt into your writing style? If so, save them into a separate folder and pull them up for reference in case you need to write something that requires a bit more formality or to people who are more senior than you. Over time, your business email writing skills should improve.

Lipstick on a Pig Is Still a Pig!

The use of clichés is part of office culture. To be honest, I've caught myself using them occasionally and didn't even know why. If you've worked in an office long enough, dropping clichés tend to happen. However, clichés are vague and don't carry much meaning. Read the letter on the next page and see if you can identify any.

Dear Employees,

I may sound like a broken record, but I would like to thank you again for putting your best foot forward this past year. We experienced a paradigm shift in strategy, leading to the best ROI we've had in decades. At the end of the day, you made a difference.

We've only just begun. We spent the year targeting low-hanging fruit, but now, it's time to think out of the box. We will be a game changer in the market as long as we manage expectations and stay results oriented. It's a win-win approach.

The CEO

Obviously, this letter is fake and lacks substance. The scary thing is, it only took a couple of minutes to create. Avoid clichés, and instead, be specific and provide examples. I think we're beating a dead horse on this subject, time to move on.

FROM THE CUBE FARM

People Notice the Shoes

Shoes reveal much about the people who wear them. They can tell us about their sense of style, attention to detail, and personality. Unfortunately, many people don't understand that. The worst offenders usually show up in offices with casual dress codes. I once saw a person in the office wear white shoes soiled with grass stains, aka, the freshly mowed grass design. I even noticed someone wear hiking boots, with crusty dirt and mud still intact. On another occasion, I saw a young lady walking out of the elevator wearing conspicuous furry boots with dangling gerbil carcasses. If you don't think people notice what you are wearing, how about considering the following examples? When I was at a training session, and the instructor asked the class what some of the best advice they received when they first started working was, a lady in the front row said, "Keep your shoes clean and polished." On another occasion, a lady complimented my shoes while we were waiting for the elevator. Apparently, she and her colleagues loved checking out the shoes the men wore around the office. So if you're a guy reading this, take notice.

Invest in shoes that are timeless in design and made with quality material. Although you will be paying more upfront, high-quality shoes last longer with proper maintenance and care. You'll save money in the long run by not having to keep replacing them.

Someone Ratted Me Out

I felt a cold coming on before leaving for work. All the signs told me to stay home, but no, I went in any way. As the first couple of hours progressed, the sniffling and sneezing evolved into a full-blown cold, and soon, the person in the adjacent cube peered over the divider and suggested that I go home. Naturally, I took her suggestion under advisement and soldiered on with my work.

Soon after, I walked past my manager, and he said that someone told him that I was not feeling too well. He told me to go home. I knew who told him that I was sick. At first, I was annoyed at my neighbor for ratting me out, but she did the right thing. I was worse the second day and stayed home. I was stubborn for not taking her advice, but most importantly, I placed my work ahead of the health of others. The last thing I wanted to do was spread germs throughout the office.

Printer Down!

I was preparing for a meeting and needed to print out a few documents. I clicked on the print icon and nothing happened. Someone walked by and noticed me at the printer trying to figure out the problem. The person said, "Oh, that printer has been down for days." My eyes rolled, and I asked, "Did anyone call this in?" He said he didn't know and had been sending his print jobs to the printer on the other side of the floor. Overhearing our conversation, my coworker called the IT Helpdesk to open a service ticket.

Hours later, a technician appeared and opened up the printer to reveal its internals. He could not find the issue and left. The printer was still non-functional. More time passed, and another technician arrived. The guy had a perplexed, but serious look on his face. He was standing in front of the printer with his arms crossed, having an internal dialogue with it. After what looked like a nod, he walked to the back of the unit and reconnected the network cable that was pulled out for some reason. Thank you, printer whisperer.

Notes

1. https://nces.ed.gov/programs/digest/d17/tables/dt17_322.10.asp
2. https://resources.workfront.com/ebooks-whitepapers/2016-state-of-enterprise-work-report-u-s-edition

AGENDA ITEM 3: I HAVE TO WORK WITH PEOPLE?

Relationship building is an overlooked skill that begins on the first day of the job. The right relationships may lead to the right career opportunities. Remember the adage of "it's not what you know but who you know?" There is much merit to that. Building relationships may come naturally to some or may be tough for others. Those who are social chameleons may have an easier time establishing work relationships over those who would rather hole up in a corner. You probably know who those people are already. There has to be a balance. Those who are extroverts may be good at relationship building, but must also prove they are strong individual contributors, and those who are introverts have to make an effort to work well with others.

"I Have Underwear Older Than You"

Born in the early 1980s, I'm what you call an old Millennial, or a Xennial (stuck somewhere between GenX and Millenials). I grew up in a time of hair sprayed big hair, Nintendo, the best Saturday morning cartoons, and MTV actually played music videos. The 1990s were spent transitioning out of the awkward teenage phase listening to Green Day, The Notorious B.I.G., and Nirvana. Since my coworkers are usually older, some have children the same age as me. A colleague once said to me early in my career, "You're only 22 years old? I have underwear older than you!" While I'm the youngest person on the team at the time of writing this book, I'm definitely no longer on the younger end of the workforce. However, I remain just as hungry as that 21-year-old who just stepped into the office for the first time, ready to climb that corporate ladder, maybe even hungrier.

Working with others across different generations is a stark contrast compared to your formal education years. You grew up and interacted with other students of similar age, in the same period of technological progress, pop-culture, economy, and political climate. However, when you start working, regardless of the type of work, you end up interacting with people of all ages. You will realize that everyone is at a different point in their lives, and have different priorities. While you may be hell-bent on making a lot of money and climbing the ladder, your older colleagues may have their sights on retirement.

The Millennials make up a large percentage of the workforce and are hungry for success. They are perceived as being lazy, unmotivated, and disengaged by the older generations, but that couldn't be further from the truth. They just work differently. In a study published in the Journal of Business and Psychology, there was no difference in work ethic across generations[1]. The Baby Boomers are winding down their careers in preparation for retirement, that is if they saved enough. The Generation X crowd is waiting for the Baby Boomers to retire so they can take over their positions.

When Millennials are not busy explaining to their older coworkers what an Instagram is, they must be learning as much from them as possible. Gen Xers and Baby Boomers are a repository of knowledge and experience to leverage. On the other end, people set in their ways after working for decades may be able to perform better by learning some new tricks and ideas from Millennials, who utilize technology to simplify and streamline their productivity. The ecosystem of younger workers replacing their older counterparts as they leave the workforce appears to be working well for now. The future will be an interesting one as artificial intelligence is rapidly advancing. Who knows? Maybe the Automaton Generation is closer than we think. We'll all be bowing to our chrome-plated robot masters soon enough.

High Five for Teamwork!

A business-oriented degree is not a requirement to work in Corporate

America. Many people end up in Corporate America with computer science, engineering, economics, math, and other types of degrees. Companies sometimes even prefer to hire people with liberal arts degrees. However, there is one common thing in school that doesn't particularly translate well to the corporate landscape. That would be the ability to work well on a team. Sure, some assignments in school require students to work in a group, but it's left up to them to choose the teammates and how to divide up the work. Teamwork seems to be appreciated more in graduate school since many students are working professionals, and it's a shame that not everyone can afford attend.

Not everyone works well on a team. Many people would rather work alone than on a team because that person believes that he or she is capable of performing better as an individual. Think back to your school days. You hate working on a team, so you go to your professor and ask for an independent project. Certainly, there is more latitude when it comes to participating in team projects in an academic setting, but you don't get to choose teammates at work.

Well, you may have gotten away with it in school by ducking out of a team project, but in the real world, working with others or being on a team is something you have to do. What are you going to do? Go to your manager and say, "Hey, I don't work well with a team. Can you give me a solo project?" Two words: career suicide.

In a study by the Office of Institutional Research of the Northern Virginia Community College, out of 1,526 respondents[2], 906 rated working with others as Very Important (highest rating), and 506 rated it as Important (second highest rating). That represents approximately 93% of respondents. In fact, in the ranking of the 17 employee characteristics and skills, Working with Others was ranked 5th[3], behind Work Ethics, Communication Abilities, Ability to Learn on the Job, and Motivation or Initiative. No doubt, it's a desirable trait and requirement many businesses look for when hiring employees. If you search "most desirable employee traits on the Internet," being a team player consistently shows up on many lists.

In another study, the National Association of Colleges and Employer's (NACE) Job Outlook for the College Class of 2013 rated the importance of being able to work in a team, near the top of the list.

Employers rate candidate soft skills/qualities (in order of importance)[4]
- Ability to verbally communicate with persons inside and outside the organization
- **Ability to work in a team**
- Ability to make decisions and solve problems
- Ability to plan, organize, and prioritize work
- Ability to obtain and process information
- Ability to analyze quantitative data
- Technical knowledge related to the job
- Proficiency with computer software programs
- Ability to create and/or edit written reports
- Ability to sell or influence others

Having smarts and other intellectual skills are essential, but communication and teamwork skills trump them. Working on a team is something that is inevitable, it's bound to happen. You can try to run away, but it'll just catch you by the ankles while you're being dragged back with your bloody fingertips scraping across the floor. Even if you're an individual contributor on a team, there will be times when you will have to communicate and work with others. If you don't like working with people, this may not be the best line of work for you. It's better to identify this weakness early on and correct it, or it may hurt your career in the future.

The People You Work with Are Not Perfect, You Included

It's easy to pass judgment on others without thinking of our own personal job-related imperfections and weaknesses. You can probably make a list of people in the office who rub you the wrong way or could improve their people skills. Guess what? Others are probably thinking the same thing about you. The workplace is a dynamic environment where you will meet new people, take on new responsibilities, and face challenges. It means there is always room for learning and improvement, especially when it comes to building relationships and working with others. We should continually be improving our people and teamwork skills. Does anything on the following list remind you of yourself when working with others?

- **You Hate People, but You Work on a Team.** You don't have to like the people you work with, but you need to learn to work well with others. Focus on the deliverables, share ideas, escalate issues, and stay engaged. Not being a team player may work against you.
- **You Have No Patience, and Everyone Else Seems to Work at a Snail's Pace.** Understand everyone has a different work pace. If you finish your tasks before others finish theirs, use the time to double-check the work or work on other tasks or projects to fill in the extra time. Ask your manager if there's more work available. If you're sitting around idle at your desk, people may think you're not working, even though you finished some time ago.
- **You Talk Too Much.** Shut up and listen to what others have to say. You might learn a thing or two. Listening is learning.
- **You Stink at Listening.** Well, that's because you talk too much. Shut up. Taking notes will help hone your listening skills when someone is speaking. Furthermore, try to use your right ear to do most of the listening. According to audiology researchers, you may remember more if you listen with the right ear [5].
- **You Are a Seat-Filler at Meetings.** You have to speak up and contribute occasionally. After all, why are you there in the first place, to fill an empty seat?
- **You Have an "I Don't Give a Crap" Attitude.** Pretend you give a crap because people will notice if you don't. If you're not engaged, then you're not an asset worth investing in. Meaning, you have no value-add for the company. It's a great way to involuntarily enroll in the employee efficiency program.
- **You Think You're Better Than Everyone Else.** There's nothing wrong with thinking it, but make sure not to come off as cocky or a know-it-all to others. It tends to drive others away. If you're good at your job, your skills will be recognized.
- **You Have Commitment Problems** You need to sit down and find out where your work bottlenecks are. Are you missing

deadlines due to too much work? Is it because the people you rely on aren't responding to you? Is it because you lack knowledge in a specific area? Is it because you procrastinate? If others depend on your work, you need to deliver on commitments.
- **You Don't Agree with How Things Are Done.** If there are opportunities to do something better, speak up. Change comes from those who take risks and see things from fresh perspectives.
- **You Are Annoyed by Stupid People.** Me too. Suck it up and deal with it.

Finding Common Ground

The typical work week is 40 hours in the United States. That means you spend a good portion of it with your co-workers. We spend so much time with them, and yet, we don't know much about them. That's because there are norms in the office that dictate to stay professional and not be too personal with each other. We are there to work, but it's important to remember that your co-workers are just like you. They also have lives outside the office and who they are in the office may not reflect who they are outside of it.

How well do you know your co-workers? Well enough to share your darkest secrets with them or the most embarrassing moments of your life? There is no question the work environment can also foster great friendships.

Relationship building with co-workers doesn't happen overnight. It's certainly not going to happen if you isolate yourself from others. Trust, communication, and commonalities are keys to forming relationships. Since people at work tend to place their best foot forward to appear professional, it's hard to get to know them on a personal level. One of your tasks is to get them to occasionally turn off 'Office Mode' to learn more about their interests. You may find out that you have the same interests as they do, which opens up new channels of communication, and hopefully, lead to better working relationships and opportunities.

Getting to know your co-workers on a more personal level requires a subtle approach. You don't want to get in their face and ask them what their interests are. The question to ask yourself is, "How do I get to know my co-workers better so that I can build stronger working relationships?" Take it slow and much will be revealed over time. The more you work with people, the more they will open up to you. People tend to overshare when asked how their weekend was, or how their day is going. It's a good a time for you to listen because when they share a bit about themselves, you may find out that you share the same interests. There may be an opportunity to say, "Hey, me too!" Getting to know your co-workers is not going to happen in a day, but over time, the more they share, and the more you share, a semi-personal relationship develops, and that can work wonders for your professional career.

An external team outing or happy hour gathering provides an excellent opportunity to interact with co-workers on a personal level. You would be surprised at how many barriers fall once people are outside of the office and have been lubed up with a bit of alcohol. Disclaimer: I am not encouraging you to get your coworkers wasted to get personal information out of them. Do pay attention to what others say, be a listener. Be mindful not to overindulge in the drinks and make a fool of yourself. Who knows, you may end up oversharing. There is probably that one person in the group who is screaming "shots, shots, shots, shots, shots, shots, shots!" Stay clear of that one. Making poor happy hour choices may forever haunt you.

No matter where you work in the world, there is one thing that usually brings strangers together. Can you guess? That would be sports. In the United States, football, basketball, and baseball reign supreme. In other parts of the world, it may be football (soccer). The power of sports has an arcane ability to create conversations in the office. "Did you see the game last night?" "Do you play fantasy football?" "Do you want to participate in the basketball office pool?" Even if you're not into sports, knowing a little bit about what's going on in the local and national sports world may give you a new avenue to open conversations with others. Use the Internet to access sports highlights and stories as it doesn't take much time to catch up on what happened.

The Gatekeepers of the Office

Know this, and know this well. The executives are not the ones in control. It's their administrative assistants who are. They are the true gatekeepers, so get on their good side. During my internship, I was assigned to work on projects most of the time, and the free time was spent helping the administrative assistant with random tasks. When I first met her, I thought an administrative assistant was there to only answer phone calls and book appointments. She was more than that. I discovered she held a fair amount of power. Since she was managing the Senior VP's calendar, she could accept or deny meeting requests from other people. Your meeting request between you and a senior manager hangs in the balance depending on your relationship with an administrative assistant. High-level managers who work together across different organizations mean that their administrative assistants know each other well. So, if you're a jerk to one, it's quite probable that another will be aware that you are a jerk as well. The gossip is real.

The Power of a Simple Hello

During the day, you're bound to walk past other people you don't know, and you may occasionally cross paths. Use these opportunities to say hello to them. Just because they're strangers doesn't mean you can't give a friendly hello. Why say hello to office strangers? Because one day, you may end up working with them on a project and upon meeting formally for the first time, the people you have been saying hello to are bound to recognize you. A simple hello can be very powerful.

Have You Tried Turning It Off and On Again?

As someone who is looked upon to help others fix computer problems, I know how frustrating it can be to help others troubleshoot a problem. IT helpdesk professionals need more appreciation for spending their days fixing computer problems. Some of them would much rather sit in a tank of piranhas wearing meat-scented underwear than work through an issue with a difficult end user.

Realize that your computer is a machine, and like any other kind of machine, it will eventually break down, stop working partially or entirely. As frustrated as you may be, don't vent on or blame the IT helpdesk person. Don't expect them to perform miracles on the fly. Give them some time to Google a solution to your problem (I'm joking, but am also dead serious about this).

Common Computer Problems. Before crying bloody murder and reaching for the phone to call the IT helpdesk for assistance, be aware that you may be able to remedy a specific problem on your own.
- Slow computer performance: Restart the computer to see if the issue clears up. If the computer is constantly slow and takes a lifetime to boot up, it may be time for a replacement.
- The computer won't start: Check if all the wires and power cables are correctly plugged in. It may sound silly, but even IT professionals sometimes forget this step.
- Peripherals such as the keyboard and mouse stop working: unplug the wires and plug them back in. If the devices are wireless, unplug the receivers, and plug them back in, and check if the batteries require replacement.
- Website isn't loading: Make sure you entered the website address accurately. Try accessing it from another computer or your smartphone to see if it loads. If you are not able to load the website across different devices, chances are, there is a problem with the website.

Make the Call. If you've tried your best to fix the problem and it still exists, it's time to call the IT helpdesk.
- Write down the description of the error or problem, especially if an error code or message appears. Take a screenshot if possible. The more information that is available to the help desk technician, the easier it will be to pinpoint the cause of the issue
- While speaking with the helpdesk technician, stay calm and be as detailed as possible and provide the error code or message if available. Don't take your frustration out on the helpdesk technician. His or her job is to gather as much information from you as much as possible. Banging on the computer and screaming at it like a crazy ape is not going to help either.
- If there is an option to do so, the helpdesk technician may ask to remotely connect into your computer to troubleshoot or fix the problem. This means the technician has full access to your computer. Save all your work before granting permission.
- Ask for an estimated time of resolution. If the issue will take a

long time to resolve and you need access to a computer, ask if a loaner is available. It's similar to dropping off your car for repairs and receiving a complimentary car for the time being.

IT helpdesk professionals spend all day resolving computer issues and based on how much work they have, may not be able to solve your computer problem immediately. Get on their bad side, and your problem ticket may end up "misplaced" within the resolution queue.

Departing Co-workers

We've probably been in a situation where a co-worker leaves for a job elsewhere. Sometimes it's hard to see them go, especially after working with them for so long. However, this is a good thing for you. It expands your network. Think about it, should you seek "greener pastures" elsewhere, you may be able to reach out to your former co-workers to keep an eye out for job opportunities at their new employer, especially if they move on to a position of power and hiring authority. Even more so, you can have them check internal job postings and refer you directly.

Usually, when I am leaving the company, co-workers are quick to ask where I am going, and also to make sure to look out for any positions that may interest them. You will be surprised at how many people are looking to change employers.

Furthermore, colleagues who depart the company due to layoffs may need job references. If someone asks you to be a reference, make sure you're comfortable with it. You may receive a call from a hiring manager or human resources employee about the applicant. Remember, you're supposed to say positive things about the person. Don't simply say how great or how nice the person is. Focus on the accomplishments, teamwork skills, and anything else that stands out. Also, the statements you make must be true.

Seeing Things Eye to Eye

When people go to another co-worker's cubicle to talk, the person in the cube usually remains seated while the visitor stands. To most people, that seems normal, but I like to give my visitors a bit of on-the-level eye to eye contact by getting out of my seat during a discussion. When people visit me, the least I can do is stop what I'm doing for a short while, and stand up. That way, it prevents the person talking "down to me."

It's a purely psychological game. If someone of higher rank walks over to your cube, stand up and talk to the person so that the higher-ranking person is not talking "down" to you. People may not be thinking that, but the action of standing up may trigger a subconscious reaction that may work in your favor. What if you end up speaking to someone, and you're the one who is standing up, and the other person is sitting? Remain standing unless you're asked to take a seat.

Transition of Work

Companies will always experience employee turnover. When an employee moves to another employer, that person's set of work and responsibilities are transferred to someone else. Sometimes, I dread it when a coworker leaves because I'll have to temporarily take on their responsibilities until a replacement steps in. It means more work for me. The hardest part is, the person has already mentally checked out after giving two weeks' notice. However, management expects the person who is leaving to transition the responsibilities to another co-worker. Transitioning work from one person to another isn't as simple as handing over a set of car keys to a new owner.

If someone who is leaving is transitioning their work to you, it may be a temporary transition until a replacement is hired, or you may end up owning it. Depending on how you look at it, it may be a good or bad thing. Looking at it from an optimistic point of view, if the transitioned work is something you haven't done before, consider it as an acquisition of a new skill. There are no rules when it comes to properly transitioning work from one person to the other, but keep the following things in mind:

Set a Transition Completion Date. Make sure everyone involved is in agreement. If the person leaves before the knowledge transfer completes, that knowledge may be lost forever.

Make a Knowledge Transfer List. For example:
- Work in progress and status.
- Upcoming deadlines and deliverables.
- Key contacts, emails, and phone numbers.
- Transfer or provide the location of documentation, such as spreadsheets, diagrams, instructions, project plans, meeting minutes, agendas, status reports, etc.
- Open issues that you need to be aware of.
- Access to certain programs and websites, emails, local and network share files.

Even if the person is leaving, ask if you can reach out for assistance if necessary. If you're the one who is leaving for another employer, do your best to transfer enough knowledge as possible. Be available for questions and guidance for a short while after leaving.

Make sure you can handle the additional workload since you still have duties to fulfill in your primary role. If you experience a "this is way over my head" moment, speak with your manager.

What's in a Name? Everything

Try to remember the names of people you meet in the office or at a work function. Chances are, you may run into them later. People love to be remembered, especially their names. It makes them feel good, and it helps them to remember you as well. It makes my day when I go to the local lunch spot, and the cashier says my name. It makes me feel important even though I'm not. There is a big difference saying "Hello John," compared to saying, "hello." It's easy to forget someone's name, especially when you're meeting a group of people at once and names are bombarded at you from all directions. Upon meeting someone new, repeat the person's name a few times in your head to help you remember. The right thing to do is to repeat that person's name when the conversation ends, for example, "Goodbye John, nice meeting you." In the event you do forget someone's name after introductions, there is no shame in asking, "I already forgot, but what is your name again?"

Use the Employee Directory to Your Advantage

A company's online employee directory usually provides basic information such as employee names, work addresses, departments, and contact information. However, if the directory also displays pictures of employees, it becomes a useful resource to leverage. For example, if you're heading to a meeting and are not familiar with the attendees, you may be able to find out what they look like, their titles, and the departments they represent. If you're starting a new job, it will be easier to associate the names with each person's face.

The employee directory may give you an idea of the organization's hierarchical structure. Search for the C-Level officers in the company, and most likely their profiles will also list the reporting structure (who reports to who). It's a great way to find out where your department stands in the organization, and also what the vertical reporting structure is. It's usually listed somewhere on the company's intranet page. If not, ask an administrative assistant since they typically have access to one.

FROM THE CUBE FARM

A Simple Hello Would've Been More Appropriate

The beginning of my internship was spent helping the administrative assistant. She often coordinated lunch meetings for the VPs. On one occasion, she asked if I wanted to call one of the VPs to coordinate one of the lunch meetings. "How hard could it be?" I thought to myself. I turned to her after the call, and she was laughing. "Did I do something wrong?" She said that I did a good job, just that next time, to not greet the person on the other line with a "Hey, what's up?"

Dr. Jekyll and Mr. Hyde

Bill and I worked on the same project. I always made an effort to say hello whenever we crossed paths, and he usually responded with an uneasy grin and indirect eye contact. Do I look weird or something? In fact, every time I saw him, he had an "I hate my job, I want to jump off a ledge," expresssion on his face.

One night after work, I was at the bar for a co-worker's farewell party and Mr. "I'm in need of an anti-depressant" shows up. But something was not right. Grumpy had some pep in his step, and he was saying hello to everyone, even me! Soon there was a cold refreshing beer in his hand, and he was on center stage telling stories and cracking jokes. I thought, "Where is Bill and what have you done to him?"

It goes to show that the people you know at work are not necessarily the same individuals when they are out of work. It was a real reverse case of Dr. Jekyll and Mr. Hyde without all the body mutations and weird noises.

Notes
1. Zabel, K.L., Biermeier-Hanson, B.B.J., Baltes, B.B. et al., Generational Differences in Work Ethic: Fact or Fiction? Journal of Business Psychology (2016)
2. Dr. George E. Gabriel, "Employee Characteristics and Skills Valued by Northern Virginia Employers," Business Needs Assessment Study No. 1. Research Report,"(2000): 14.
3. Gabriel, "Employee Characteristics and Skills Valued by Northern Virginia Employers," 7.
4. NACE, The Job Outlook for the College Class of 2013
5. https://www.sciencedaily.com/releases/2017/12/171206090611.htm

AGENDA ITEM 4: BE SELFISH ABOUT YOUR CAREER

Think all the way back to your middle and high school days. Remember when your voice started to crack and hair began to grow in funny places? That was a crazy time. Anyway, as awkward or normal your teenage years were, you probably had a guidance counselor to help guide you through all aspects of personal, social, and academic growth. The end goal was to get you into the college or trade school of your choice. In colleges and universities, there usually is a career services office that holds job fairs, mock interview workshops, and provides counselors to help guide students down a specific career path. At times, it felt like those counselors had a stake in the career choices we made. As you have already realized, once you entered the real world, there is no guidance or career counselor to lean on. You're on your own. Sure you can argue that your manager and co-workers are "there for you when you need them," however, there is only one major stakeholder when it comes to your career, you. With that said, learn to be selfish about your career. It's every man and woman for themselves when it comes to climbing the corporate ladder, you have to knock some people off on the way up (metaphorically speaking that is, please don't physically beat your coworkers). They'll do the same thing to you if given the opportunity.

Take advantage of any employer perks and benefits to gain new skills and knowledge. Sometimes you have to take what's not given to you. Look for opportunities to make your position your own. There may be ways to leverage it to your advantage, whether it's for moving up at your current employer, or for setting up for a better position elsewhere. If you plan to surf the Internet and be paid to poop, then maybe a dead-end job is right for you. Don't be mad if you're passed over for a promotion though.

Is the Company a Good Fit for You?

During a job interview, the hiring manager is deciding whether you will be a good fit for the department and the company. You may also interview with potential teammates or business partners who have a stake in the position. On the opposite end of the table, it's your job to find out if the position and company is a good fit for your work style and career, but it all depends on the type of employee you are. Are you the one who goes with the flow or one who changes the direction of it?

I was in a meeting with a couple of co-workers, and our work-related discussion took off on a tangent to one about job satisfaction. One co-worker was new to the job, and the other, a twenty-year veteran of the company. I didn't speak much as I was enjoying their discussion from the sidelines. What I heard was enlightening. The conversation went something like this:

New guy: "You have been working here for a while. Tell me the truth, what is your job satisfaction here?"

Veteran: "I'm never bored. I started here on the bottom rung, learned everything on the job, and worked my way up. I like it here. The work is challenging, and I feel that I have made a difference."

New guy: "It's a bit different here. It's a smaller shop, and I don't know where to start. Our manager doesn't give us much guidance, aside from reviewing some of my documents and telling me to keep the content simple."

Veteran: "That's because you won't get any guidance from the manager. You were hired as the expert, and you are expected to own the role. When someone asks about the product or process you support, all eyes are on you to provide the answer. You are empowered here."

New guy: "So you're saying, that I can create new processes where necessary."

Veteran: "That's right, you were hired to fill that gap. The manager is looking to you for results. You have the chance to create something that has never been done before. Take advantage of this culture. Not many places give you the freedom to work with minimal supervision. And guess what, the company will adopt whatever you create as long as it's aligned with the organization's goals."

New guy: "I see, so you can create stuff for the better, and the company will adopt it."

Veteran: "Look, you need to decide if this is the right company for you. If you want to work in an environment where you just go with the flow and just be one of the drones, then this is not the company for you. If you want to be able to create change and have the feeling that what you do here actually matters, then this the place to do so. Look at this guy (the Veteran points at me). He's taking full advantage of his entrepreneurial spirit to change things around here because he is empowered to do so. I know he's taking any opportunity to strengthen up his resume, and I don't blame him."

New guy: "I understand now. I can dictate the terms here. That's exciting."

It seemed the new guy was having a bit of trouble adjusting to his new role. As with joining or changing employers, there is an adjustment period, and how long that takes depends on the individual and the company. Sometimes people are not able to make the adjustment and eventually end up someplace else, back with their previous employer, or worse, unemployed. Many factors may affect the adjustment period.

Examples include:

- Having the ability to absorb a significant amount of new information with a limited amount of time.
- Getting used to the new pace of work.
- Continuing the work left by the previous person who held the position without any guidance.
- Understanding how the company operates.
- Getting to know the teammates and working on a new team.
- Understanding the manager's management style.
- Assimilating into the corporate culture.
- Struggling to adapt because the job description was different from the actual job.

You Are Not Your Worst Enemy

Look in the mirror. See that person staring back at you? That's your worst enemy, the one you must compete with to succeed. If you punch it, it'll punch right back. Well, that's a crock of motivational BS. I learned early on in business school that the competition wasn't with myself. No recruiter is ever going to be impressed that I had to take calculus twice and studied my butt off in order meet the minimum requirements for applying to business school and got accepted. There was one individual in business school who felt the classes weren't challenging enough and took on a semester-long private study class to help one of the professors with his research. Meanwhile, I only passed with a decent grade in operations management due to the grading curve. There were also those who had the gift of gab to impress the recruiters and job interviewers. They had a sharp tongue, seeming able to convince anyone with words and charisma. And of course, there were those who would lie, cheat, and manipulate their way to get in a position of good grades and standing. I was not like any of them and realized how outclassed I was by the middle of the program's first semester. I knew, no matter how hard I tried, there would be people who were smarter and better than me, but that didn't mean I didn't deserve to be successful.

Students interested in Finance, Marketing, Accounting, Management, and Management Science degrees had to apply to the business school during their second year and be accepted by the review board. Most of the applicants had to meet the minimum GPA requirement, write an essay and list extracurricular activities. Either you got accepted or ended up declaring a major in Economics, the backup business major.

The competition amongst business school students intensified by the simple rule of supply and demand. The demand for summer internships and full-time positions is greater than what is available in the job market. While everyone may seem to get along on the outside, deep down inside, we would take any opportunity to one-up each other should one ever cross our paths. I got into Corporate America through networking and had the right set of technical skills that the company was looking for, that was my leverage. And guess what? I managed to score an internship while some of those who outclassed me didn't. So what if I wasn't the brightest in the class? There is more than one way to skin a cat.

In the real world, you will be competing with those who are younger, older, smarter, hold more degrees, have more experience, and engage in questionable business ethics. The question is, how will you use your hard skills, soft skills, and office know-how to stay competitive? It's still about supply and demand. The supply of available promotions, raises, and bonuses are limited, yet everyone in the company expects to receive a promotion, raise, and performance bonus. Simply put, there isn't enough of that stuff to go around for everybody. The same goes for applying for jobs, only this time, you don't know how many people are competing with for one available job position. Your goal is to prove your worth to the company so that you're considered for a promotion and receive a higher percentage of monetary compensation over others. On two occasions, my managers fought to give me bigger bonuses, and it worked. A manager who looks out for you is a valuable thing for your career, and these are the people who you stay in contact with. A former manager did all he could to get me promoted, but circumstances at the executive level made things difficult and kept dragging on. A headhunter contacted him to apply for a management position elsewhere, but he felt that it fitted my career aspirations better and encouraged me to apply instead. My manager simply told me, "this may be a challenging role, but you're ready." I got the job and for the first time, held a position where I called the shots.

However, you need to be willing to compete. If you end up sitting at your desk all day satisfied with your work, not thinking about doing more, then maybe you've attained work nirvana. For the rest of us who are bloodthirsty, fortifying your job-related skills through obtaining advanced degrees, leadership training, and certifications will take you to a level of being able to compete with others.

Be Prepared to Pay Your Dues

The hardest part of being an entry-level employee at any corporation is the grunt work. You're armed with a college degree and find yourself running reports and performing other types of menial tasks, aka, busy work. There is another term for it, but I'll keep that one to myself. At one company, my first year was spent updating employee contact information, formatting documents, and updating verbiage across multiple documents. It was so boring that I almost quit. I felt overqualified for the position and compared myself to a mindless, keyboard-tapping ape. However, when I read my annual performance review, the manager wrote that I was an "effective worker who made few mistakes that didn't require rework." He told me to stay the course and to keep up the good work. The following year, I held more responsibilities on top of the grunt work. When one of the team leads left the company, I absorbed some of his duties. At the next performance review, I was promoted to a lead and received a generous salary bump. Two years later, I made Associate Director. The experience set me up for new opportunities outside of the company, which I took advantage of and changed industries for a more challenging role.

Sometimes we are stuck with boring and mundane assignments. However, you have to prove that you're more than competent at those assignments. I remember watching a documentary on Japanese food and the apprentice complained to the chef that he was sick of washing and folding hand towels. The chef looked at the apprentice's shoddy work and said, "How can I trust you with the food when you can't even properly clean and fold the hand towels?" That quote has stuck with me ever since. If you're unable to handle the boring tasks, how are you going to handle the challenging ones?

Status Reports

A weekly status report is a powerful tool in your career advancement inventory. You are not only providing a status of your work and progress to management, but also to yourself. Even if you're not required to provide status reports, it doesn't hurt to write them away. Below are the reasons you should get into the habit of creating weekly status reports.

Create a Paper Trail. It shows a trail of work that you have completed since day one on the job. It'll give you a perspective on your growth or stagnation in your position.

Use as Reference Material. It serves as a source of reference for ad-hoc status report requests from management because you will never know when you will have to create a monthly, quarterly, or annual report on the work you have completed. It also serves as great resume building fodder.

Document Accomplishments. A former colleague at work was on the hunt for opportunities outside of the company, and she shared this great tip with me. She told me to keep an accomplishments folder for every job that I held. It's a compilation of kudos and congratulatory emails from peers, managers, and customers on past accomplishments. It serves as excellent reference material for resumes and job interviews. Not to mention it's a great confidence booster and a reminder of the value that you bring to the companies you worked at. It is also an excellent place to store your offer letters, as well as documentation of promotion and salary raise history. Wish I did that sooner.

Create Status Reports for Management. The amount of detail in a status report is going to vary depending on who receives the report. If it's for your direct manager, then something detailed is always good, but if the report gets passed along to the higher-ups, maybe a one-page summary report with simple colored charts and graphs to show what projects are on time or behind schedule may be enough.

Getting Too Attached to Your Work

It's not easy to give up work that we've been responsible for to someone else. You have owned a particular responsibility for some years and are given new ones because you either got promoted, or someone sees potential in you. However, you're going to have to transition your old responsibilities to someone else on the team. For example, Project Puppy is your assignment. Your goal is to raise the dog to adulthood. You spend the next two years raising the dog. It's your…wait for it… pet project. One day, your manager comes to you and says, "You've done a great job raising the dog, I'm going to give you something more challenging. I'm going to give you Project Platypus, but you have to give up the dog to another co-worker to care from now on." How would you react?

We get attached to particular types of work, especially the ones we create and own. You've spent years developing and managing Project Puppy, and everyone knows that it's your project. To keep growing in your job, Project Puppy has to be transferred to someone else to make room for Project Platypus. You question if the person taking over the work is as competent as you. Will the quality of work be worse, the same, or even better? (Can this person take care of my dog as well as I can?) Can I trust this person with this work? (Did I leave my dog in good hands?) These questions will fill your mind, but don't look at it as a loss. Look at it as a skill set that you have permanently added to your professional profile and it opens you up for more opportunities, like raising a platypus.

Be Proactive About Receiving Feedback

Receiving feedback is essential for career growth. If you could be doing something better, wouldn't you want to know? There are usually two periods of the year when employees receive performance feedback from their managers. The first is the mid-year assessment and the second is the end of year review. These methods for providing feedback are antiquated. Instead of waiting for feedback, be proactive and ask for it consistently throughout the year.

There is no way to weasel out of the review periods. However, would you rather sit in a performance review where the manager is giving you feedback on how to improve, or on how much you have developed over the year? The two conversations are night and day.

Receiving criticism, constructive or not, may feel like a personal attack. Yes, it's a difficult pill to swallow when someone tells us there's room for improvement. It's an opportunity for you not to act out or defend your actions, but to become a listener and take constructive feedback with a grain of humility. Ask how you can improve based on the feedback as it may lead to new learning and training opportunities. It will also show a level of maturity on your part.

Finding Your Management Style

There is no shortage of management books available on the market. If you're an analyst or in a similar position, you probably don't plan to be one for the rest of your career. Eventually, aspirations of becoming a manager and having a team or department of your own will come into the picture. There is just one problem. You have never been a manager before. How does one become a manager? Ah, maybe the answer lies in reading a bunch of management books.

Well, reading "how to be a manager" books is not going to turn you into a manager overnight. The books provide you with ideas and guidance that can be best suited in helping you find your management style. What is your management style? That is something you will have to figure out.

At the very least, you're already managing yourself, and your manager (We'll get into that later). Also, you're managing your work. You are responsible for the quality of the work and making deadlines. Keep in mind that everyone's management style is going to be different. What works for your manager may not work for you. Don't try to force yourself to be a specific type of manager. It should come naturally and match your personality. For example, if you're more of a laid-back type of person, don't try to be aggressive or micro-manage. You can spend all day reading management books, but in the end, do what feels best for you.

The High Potential Employee

Each employee is different in regards to intellect, motivation, work ethic, and career aspiration. It comes to no surprise that some employees outperform others. There are the worker bees, who come in every day to do the same job to earn a paycheck. Then there are others who come in every day to take the necessary steps to ascend to the next rung on the corporate ladder.

During the company's annual performance review period, managers rate their employees on a number scale. Most employees will receive an average rating just for doing their job. The ones who consistently rate above average may be identified as high potentials (HiPos). While employees with above average ratings will typically receive higher bonus and raise percentages than those who are rated average, there is more to it. These are the employees who have proven themselves over and over again, and management has taken notice.

HiPos are individuals that employers want to invest in. That means employers are willing to spend resources, usually time and money to train those individuals into leaders, or to enhance their skillset. Employers also see it as a strategy to retain such employees. Pay them well, and provide them with career growth opportunities so that they won't jump ship. However, this is a double-edged sword as there is a risk the employees may change employers after completing a particular course of training.

So, if high potential employees receive extra consideration regarding leadership training, promotions, skills-related training, and more opportunities to take on new challenges, what about the average worker bees? Obviously, they aren't provided the same opportunities to grow. Budget constraints limit training opportunities for all employees, and it makes sense for employers to invest their money in those who will show a high rate of return. It's the same for making financial investments is it not? We prefer to invest in financial vehicles that will give us the best rate of return with as little risk as possible. Why would an employer send a low performing employee to leadership training if that person is not able to perform the tasks the job calls for?

What does it take to become a high potential employee? Being good at your job isn't enough. How do you convince management that you are an employee worth investing in? Well, there's no magical formula, but those who are identified as a high potential employees have the following traits and behaviors in common.

They Talk to Their Managers About Career Growth. This part is critical, and perhaps the easiest first step. You need to have someone be your champion. Talk to your manager to see if you can partake in leadership opportunities or work on challenging projects to prove your worth. If you feel you're lacking a specific skill or would like to pursue a certification, ask for training support to show that you are willing to learn and to improve your skills. Also, it's important that your manager is supportive of your career growth. If you're ever in a position where the manager does not have your best interests in mind, it may be a waste of time.

They are Willing to Prove Their Worth. You must produce high-quality work. If your manager is always second-guessing your work, then you have a long way to go. Deliver your work on time and don't make many mistakes. Prove that you can work independently without needing supervision or having your hand held.

They Show Passion. As simple as it is, you have to show that you are enthusiastic about your job, that you believe in it, and show a high level of energy of doing so.

They Are Visible. Get to know everyone the best as you can and let them know what you do and how your work contributes to the organization. Dress well, say hello to others, have good office manners, and present confidence. Sitting at your desk all day and not interacting with others places you at a disadvantage. Remember, out of sight, out of mind. Think of it as marketing yourself.

They Take Initiative. Stepping up to new challenges or sharing ideas that could solve a problem shows you are willing to do more than just what the job entails. This shows forward thinking skills. Is there a certain process that can be improved? Present a solution. Is there a way to cut costs while retaining or improving the current rate of output? Present a solution.

They Are Strong Individual Contributors and Team Players. You need to prove that you can excel independently without much guidance and also be a worthy contributor on a team. Offer help if you have the bandwidth and the know-how.

They Have the Capacity to Learn. You have to show that not only are you are willing and able to learn, but also have the ability to grow from learning and apply new skills.

It doesn't matter how old you are or how long you have been working, you can become a high potential employee if you're willing to invest the time and effort into developing your skills and growing your career. All of the effort has to come from you. No one's going to come to you and ask if you want to become a high potential employee. With that said, future success isn't guaranteed. It's not easy to sustain high performance. The possibility of failure or not meeting expectations will always be there. However, since high potential employees have proven to be successful in the past, they are people that management is willing to bet on in becoming future leaders.

The Continued Pursuit of Knowledge

Most entry-level positions require a college degree. Years of formal education placed you at the top of the educational hierarchy, and now you get to start at the dirty bottom rung of the corporate ladder. However, solely holding an undergraduate degree may limit your climb to the top. These days, positions in management and leadership often require a graduate degree or a professional certification in the related field. Fortunately, many companies are willing to invest in their employees' growth to ensure that they have the best talent available. You need to take advantage of such opportunities.

Training Opportunities. These are no-brainers. Sign up for these as much as possible to fortify, expand, or to acquire new skills. Take that new training completion certificate and tack it on your cube wall.

Tuition Reimbursement/Discounts. Companies may provide their employees with discounted or free education to obtain an advanced degree. Depending on the company, employees may attend a school of their choice, or attend regional colleges or universities that the firm has partnered with. If you have the time and the motivation, take full advantage of this perk.

Conferences. Industry or skill specific conferences are great venues for keeping professionals up to date with the latest industry trends, strategies, and products. They may even award continuing education units (CEUs) for attendance. While there will be companies that are trying to sell their products, there should be opportunities to see what your peers are doing on their end. Conferences also present great opportunities to meet new people and expand your professional network. Don't forget to bring business cards.

Certifications. Holding certifications or qualified designations in your profession may not only give you a salary and career advancement advantage over peers who don't, but also may be a requirement for specific job positions and employers. Many certifications need to be renewed periodically by obtaining CEUs through meeting requirements issued by the governing body of the certification.

Obtaining certification requires a substantial amount of cost and time commitment. For example, financial analysts who pursue the prestigious Chartered Financial Analyst (CFA) designation have to complete three levels of exams over several years. The pass rate for the first level exam is less than 50%. Of course, not all certification requirements are that rigorous. It depends on your profession.

The cost of obtaining a certification ranges from hundreds to thousands of dollars. The best method of paying for it is with someone else's money, that is, your employer's. If you can have your certification and annual dues paid for, it's a no-brainer, go for it. Below is a list of standard certifications:

- Certified Public Accountant (CPA)
- Chartered Financial Analyst (CFA)
- Project Management Professional (PMP)
- Certified Information Systems Professional (CISSP)
- Cisco Certified Network Professional (CCNP)

Keep Up with the Industry. Whether you're a marketing analyst, financial analyst, business analyst, IT analyst, or in management, chances are, you're working in a particular industry or specialty. It means there are many others out there like you. There are bound to be clubs and associations that give people in the same line of work a forum to talk, share ideas, and to see what the next big thing is. Social websites such as Facebook and LinkedIn have professional associations and groups that seek followers and members. The LinkedIn groups are great resources for sharing ideas and establishing new network contacts.

If the company can send you to conferences or training, take advantage as often as possible. Some companies may not have the budget to send their employees to conferences or training, and employees may have to pay out of pocket. It's not an ideal circumstance, but if it's a must attend, and you know that you will benefit, go for it.

Trade publications that are specific to your line of work or industry may also be helpful. Many of these publications don't require subscription fees. Look to subscribe to electronic publications as well as those that are in print.

MOOC It Up. The acronym stands for Massive Open Online Course. Many top-tier universities such as Harvard, MIT, and UPenn Wharton offer these courses. While some are self-paced, instructors also lead some. These courses are usually free, and the difficulty ranges from beginner to advanced on just about any subject. If you have the time and the aptitude to learn something new, take a look at what MOOCs have to offer. While these are great for continued professional development, these courses are not a substitute for an actual degree or certification. Having completed a MOOC offered by Harvard won't make you a Harvard graduate.

Making Mistakes is Ok…As Long as It's Not a Big One

Throughout my career, I've made mistakes. Most were minor, but I definitely had some "Oh crap, I'm getting fired!" moments. The usual advice I get from managers regarding mistakes is, "It's ok to make mistakes, but don't make the same mistake twice." The more I reflect on that statement, the more I try not to be a wise-ass. So, is it ok to keep making different mistakes? What if I make a mistake that could mess a bunch of stuff up? My takeaway is, if you make a mistake, hope it doesn't place your job in jeopardy.

Not all mistakes are created equal. Typo and spelling errors are common and the easiest to prevent. However, if you consistently make typos, it may tell others that you don't bother to double-check the work or don't pay attention to detail. The worst typo is mistyping someone's name in an email. It makes you feel like a crappy person, right? I mean, you can't even type in a name correctly. Then there are calculation mistakes, depending on what the calculations are for, can have severe consequences. Always pay extra attention to the math and formulas. Remember what happened in *Office Space* [Spoiler Alert] when the character Michael Bolton miscalculated the placement of a decimal point in a computer program that was designed to steal money from the company?

If you know you caused something catastrophic, quickly inform management because they may have encountered something similar in the past, or will be able to reach out to the right resources to remedy the situation. Hiding a mistake or trying to blame others is the worst thing you can do. Sitting on the mistake and letting it snowball isn't recommended either. Remember, the work you do has a certain level of impact at the company, and there are no redos for big mistakes. Own up to your mistake and hope for the best. You're a professional now.

Office Street Cred

For this section, I felt it would be more effective to deliver the message in the form of a story. Once upon a time, there were two senior business analysts named John and Stan. Both report to their manager, Jane. John is punctual, always in the office by 9 AM and leaves at 5 PM. He gives 100% on the job and produces high-quality work. Stan, however, arrives to work two hours before and leaves two hours later than John every day. You probably think that Stan is the harder worker, based on the fact that Stan spends more time in the office. However, his work output is half of John's.

Jane recommends John for a promotion, but her manager Paul is challenging it. He believes Stan deserves the promotion over John. Jane is confused since Stan is an average employee at best. Paul explains that Stan is always first in the office and usually the last to leave, more employees need to be more like him. She explains John is more efficient and produces higher quality work, hence the promotion recommendation.

The importance of perception management and visibility plays a vital role in your job. Together, they help to establish your "office street cred." Stan is perceived to be a hard worker, and John's work is not visible beyond his manager. Perception management focuses on active and passive actions that imprint an image of yourself onto others. In other words, it's about managing how others perceive you. If you keep missing deadlines, others will perceive you to be unreliable. If you act like an idiot, guess what? Others will see you as an idiot. On the other hand, positive perceptions may help you to gain visibility in the organization.

Visibility has two components: your physical presence in the organization, and the visibility of your work and its value. How often do you walk by or pass certain people in the office and know exactly who they are and what they do? They are the rock stars of the workplace, yet, they have no idea who you are. Those people have high presence visibility. Is your work visible to other middle and senior level managers? If your contributions are visible to the right people, and they notice the value of them, it may increase the chances of career advancement.

Increasing visibility may be difficult due to your job position. For example, what if your role doesn't interact with others and the work produced never leaves the confines of the department? Look for other avenues in the company to gain visibility. Participating in company-sponsored charity and volunteering events provides an excellent opportunity to meet employees in other departments. You will instantly improve your visibility with the added benefit that the people you will meet will most likely be from other parts of the organization. Get out there, meet new people, and let them know who you are and what you do!

Back to the story of John and Stan. What steps could Jane have taken to justify her recommendation for John's promotion? Jane should highlight the team's accomplishments to her manager throughout the year and give credit to whom it's due. What could John have done to increase his visibility? Perhaps, John should have asked Jane how his work is visible to others in the organization. To put it another way, are his hard efforts recognized beyond his manager? If not, are there opportunities for his contributions to be more visible in the organization?

Setting Goals, a Necessary Evil

Once a year, I feel a disturbance in the Force. As if all the employees in the company are cringing in disgust at once. It happens right after the human resources department sends the email about setting annual performance goals. You're probably thinking, "I do great work, setting goals is a waste of time." The company's performance management process provides a standardized methodology for assessing employee performance through goal setting. It's a barometer, essentially the report card, that results in assigning employees a rating. For example, if employees are rated on a scale from 1 to 4, the details for each rating may be similar to the one I made up below:

- **1 Rating:** Employee is underperforming, may require probation until performance improves. In a nutshell, this employee sucks.
- **2 Rating:** Employee is valued and performs as expected, aka, the average employee who does no more, and no less. In a nutshell, this employee is average, don't expect great things.
- **3 Rating:** Employee occasionally outperforms, is a high-potential employee. This person is a valued contributor and does more than expected. In a nutshell, this one has potential, let's keep an eye this one.
- **4 Rating:** Employee consistently outperforms, is god-like. The unicorns of the company. Rare and hard to believe there are people who perform at this level. In a nutshell, where can we find more employees like these? Is cloning an option?

Even though the goal setting method isn't perfect and many variables may affect an employee's rating, such as quality of work, organizational visibility, and perception, it's one of those necessary evils in life, like flossing before bedtime.

Goals tend to trickle down from the top. For example, the Chief Operations Officer has to reduce operating expenses in the company by at least 10% by the end of the fiscal year. How will this goal be met? This goal will trickle down to all the departments.

The requirements for developing goals vary for each company. Some companies may only require high-level goals, and some may require detailed goals. A couple of companies I worked at utilized the S.M.A.R.T. goal development guidelines. The variation of S.M.A.R.T. that I'm familiar with is that goals need to be Specific, Measurable, Achievable, Relatable, and Timely. Below is an example of how developing a goal with the SMART method works. Let's go back to the previous example.

Manager Lauren in the procurement department requires each of her direct reports to develop a goal that will align with the COO's goal of reducing operating costs. What could her direct reports do to cut costs? Drink one less cup of coffee per day? Reduce paper printouts by 10%? Steal 50% fewer office supplies? If only it were that simple. One of Lauren's direct reports, Jake, has an idea. He wants to replace the aging procurement system that costs the company $50,000 annually to run. The contract renewal period is coming up, and he knows of a new product that not only is much better but will also reduce cost. Let's develop the goal for Jake with the guidance of S.M.A.R.T.

- **Specific:** Replace the aging procurement system with one that is newer and will significantly reduce departmental overhead.
- **Measurable:** Department cost savings of at least 25% in the first year, 30% in the years after. Reduce manual processes by 35%.
- **Achievable:** As great at the goals sounds, is it a goal that can be met and not something that's so far out of reach, that it sets Jake up for failure? If Jake fails to deliver, it may impact his performance rating.
- **Relatable**: Increases job efficiency, reduces busy work, and reduces operating cost.
- **Timely:** Completion by the end of the fiscal third quarter.

Jake's S.M.A.R.T. Goal Is: Replace the old procurement system with a new one by the end of the fiscal third quarter to reduce recurring annual costs by at least $12,500 in the first year, and $15,000 in the years after. The new system will also reduce busy work by 35% through automation.

Speak to your manager about adding a goal for personal development. For example, if you want to develop leadership skills, ask to see if there is an opportunity to take leadership training. You could also work towards getting certified in your profession or attend industry conferences and seminars. There may be times when high-level organizational goals are automatically assigned to all employees.

The Thing About Job Titles

Do job titles matter? It depends on whom you ask. Most people fall into two categories: Those who value a title more than anything else, and those who don't care what they're called. As a former co-worker once said to me, "They can call me a janitor as long as the paychecks keep coming."

I remember the day when a project manager received her promotion to vice president. Her manager said, "Well, you may not be getting a raise, but you will have more responsibilities." As an intern witnessing the event, I thought, "That's a crappy promotion." I wondered if he was joking. He wasn't.

It was not until later in my career did I realize that promotions are not limited to raises. The title change may align the employee on a particular management path at the company. Extra perks such as additional vacation, stock purchase opportunities, and profit sharing may be available to employees at certain position levels.

There are companies out there that place a creative spin on job titles. For example, the title of Customer Support Representative may be called "Chief People Pleaser" instead. Having a particular title on the resume may open doors to new opportunities and higher-ranking positions. However, while it may get you noticed, you still have to prove your worth. Having a good title can only carry you so far. I interviewed a candidate to fill a senior information technology analyst position. He was a senior information technology analyst at his current employer, which would have been a lateral move for him. However, even though the two companies used the same job title, the expectations and experience required for the position couldn't have been more different. To me, his senior analyst role was more aligned to that of a junior analyst role.

If you expect to reach a particular title by a certain age, be realistic. Chase opportunities that will provide you with the best learning experiences and challenges instead of titles. No rule states what rank you should be at by a certain age. Everyone develops at a different pace. Other factors such as competition, industry, and salary bands may affect the title you receive. Keep in mind a title's rank in the organizational hierarchy may differ from one company to another, especially within middle management. There is no standard for defining titles and their rank. Take the title of Vice President, for example; it may be an upper management position at one company and a much lower one at another. This also means the salary bands will differ. According to some person I met at a conference, "everyone's a VP at a bank."

Be defined by the work you do, so that you earn that promotion and title that comes along with it. You're not going to hear, "John does good work because he's a VP." You're going to hear, "John does good work because he cares about his clients and secures more accounts than anyone else in the division. His position is well-deserved."

In 2015, Zappos, the online shoe retailer, kicked the hierarchical organizational model out the door and adopted one known as a holacracy. There are no job titles in a holacracy. The goal is to empower employees to make decisions on their own without having to wait for permission from their managers. Employees who did not agree with the change had the option to be bought out; 14% of the company's 1,600 employees took the offer.[1] If you're obsessed with having a prestigious title, you could start a small LLC as the only employee, and name yourself CEO, Chairman, Founder, and President.

Keep the Résumé Updated

While most of us usually update our resumes when we decide to look for a new job or if a headhunter is requesting one, no rule says we cannot update it at any time. The best time to update the resume is after the completion of a major project or the assignment of new responsibilities. Years may pass between updating the resume and what happens is hours, if not days, are spent updating it when an unexpected job opportunity presents itself.

Using the status reports will help to filter out the significant accomplishments from the minor ones. Keeping the resume updated will also help you keep track of the positions you have held and what you have accomplished in them. If a random job opportunity comes up, you won't have to worry too much about getting it ready. If you have a professional online profile, keep that updated regularly as well.

Job Hunting, No One Has to Know

There are many reasons for changing employers. You may keep having, "I don't get paid enough to do this crap" moments, or that management doesn't have your best interests in mind. Maybe you feel it's time to move on. Whatever the reason, the best time to search for a new job is when you already have one. Employers are more likely to hire employed people. Use this to your advantage if you're thinking of making a move. However, you wouldn't want your current employer to find out that you're in the job market for a new position elsewhere. What to do?

Resist the urge to job search and apply for positions at work. Even if your manager doesn't notice you're in the hunt and using company resources to do so, someone else may take notice and start spreading the news around the office. If you cannot resist the urge, search discreetly on your smartphone in the bathroom while you take care of business. This way you could be paid to poop and search for a new job. According to the website TalentWorks, the chances of receiving a job interview goes up by five times if you apply for a job between the hours of 6 AM and 10 AM during the employer's timezone[2]. The website also states to not apply after 4 PM. I'm a bit skeptical since one time I applied for a job on a Friday at 7 PM. I was on a plane the very next week for a job interview, and I got the job. Here's the thing, if your resume fulfills almost every checkmark regarding what the job posting is looking for, and you have the right keywords, you should have no problem landing an interview, regardless of the time you apply.

Hopefully, you will land an interview, and when you do, the first will most likely be a phone screening with a human resources representative. These types of interviews are usually held during business hours focusing on general and behavioral questions. Avoid taking the call at your desk. Instead, book a small conference room in a quiet area that has good cellular reception, or go to a private area where you cannot be disturbed or overheard.

You pass the phone screen and are sent to the next round, the in-person interviews. The prospective employer wants you to interview sometime during the weekday between 9 AM to 5 PM. You know what that means, you will have to take time off from work. The easiest way is to take the whole day off. If you can only afford to be away for half a day (morning or afternoon), don't show up or return to work in your interview attire. It's a dead giveaway.

Always save a couple of vacation or paid-time-off (PTO) days for such occasions. You may encounter multiple-round interviews, so having a few extra days to burn is a good idea. Or, you could just call out sick *cough, cough* if that doesn't raise any suspicion.

Stuff Happens, Be Prepared

It's time to get a bit more serious and talk about your personal safety at work. After your home, the workplace is likely the place you spend the most time. Like anywhere else, accidents happen, and you could face a life-threatening situation. Companies usually don't spend enough time discussing life-safety procedures with employees. If you're a consultant, you most likely won't go through employee orientation. While companies usually perform fire evacuation and shelter-in-place drills, they are often performed a couple of times a year or less. That means, unless you participate in a safety drill on your first day of work, you will have to wait until the next one is scheduled, but things could happen between now and later.

If you're not familiar with how life-safety procedures work at the office you work in, find out as soon as possible. For example, do you need to dial an extra number to get an outside line before dialing 911? Do you know where the evacuation routes and stairwells are in the building? Do you have any idea where the assembly points are? What if the closest exit is blocked, do you know where the next one is located? Is there an evacuation team assigned to the floor? Check if the information provided is in the company's employee handbook. If not, talk to someone in the human resources department to point you in the right direction.

We live in a time where active shootings seem to be taking place more than ever. While it's rare that you will find yourself that type of situation, it's important to know how to respond if it does occur at your place of work. We see it on the news all the time, yet when the subject is brought up in the workplace, people tend ostrich (stick their heads in the ground and try to ignore the issue). Active shooting events can happen anywhere and ignoring the topic is not going to make it go away. No doubt it's a sensitive subject, but companies are taking notice more than ever and may have active shooter response procedures available. Again, ask the human resources team if the company has information or provides training regarding active shooter situations.

Employee Perks

Many companies, especially major corporations offer their employees certain perks. They may offer discount retail shopping rates, free access to certain forms of entertainment, free admission to local attractions for being a corporate sponsor, and even incentives for continuous education. Some of these perks may add up to significant savings.

Culture Up. Discounts or free admission to local museums and other local area attractions are always a good deal. Don't pass these up if you're really into that sort of stuff since admission fees tend to cost an arm and a leg. Depending on the company, corporate passes may allow employees to bring along a guest or more.

Discount Retail Programs. Companies are often able to pass on hardware and software discounts to their employees based on their relationships with key vendors. Some may even offer discounts to other retailers that sell clothing and services such as reduced mobile phone plans. While some of the offered discounts may be significant, it doesn't hurt to shop around online first. Deals found on the Internet may be better than those offered by the company, and the corporate discounts usually don't stack onto Internet discounts and vice versa.

Start Building That Nest Egg as Early as Possible

A wise, old walrus[3] once told me, "Don't do what I did. You are young, save as much money as you can now!" The typical retirement savings vehicles companies provide to their employees are either pensions or a type of employee defined contribution plan, such as a 401k. A 401k is an employer-sponsored retirement savings plan where the employee can invest in funds. Fund performance is affected by the stock and bonds market. An entry-level employee I spoke with had no idea what affected 401k performance. A percentage of the employee's paycheck is used to invest in the funds. In this day and age, pensions are going away for 401ks, but some sectors still have them. Some companies provide a little extra incentive for employees who participate in the company's 401k retirement savings program, known as matching. This is how it works:

Your annual salary is $60,000.00. The company is going to match 5% ($3000.00) of your salary, dollar for dollar, as long as you place 10% ($6,000) of your annual salary into its 401k savings program. The company match is essentially free money, and it can help with the volatility of the market. The amount is automatically deducted in equal installments from each paycheck to purchase the funds you allocated in your portfolio.

Picking and choosing the funds to invest in is completely up to you and positive returns on investment are not guaranteed. The amount of money matched on a 401k depends solely on the employer. Some match dollar for dollar and some match 50 cents for each dollar invested up to a certain percentage.

It's also a good idea to see if you need to be vested until you receive the match from your employer. For example, even though the company has been matching the money you have been placing into the 401k, the matched money is not yours until you have met the minimum vesting requirements, which may mean you have to work at the company for a certain number of years. If you leave the company before meeting the vesting requirements, you may not receive any of the 401k matches or only a percentage of it.

If you're still not convinced that you should start putting money away as early as possible, maybe the concept of compound interest will. The rule of 72 will be used to show how long it takes to double your money based on a given interest rate, also known as the rate of return. To see how long it takes to double your money, just divide 72 by the interest rate. Let's say you presently have $10,000 in the account and assuming a constant 8% interest rate (72/8 = 9). It will take nine years to double the $10,000. The following table shows how much the money will grow over time.

Present Balance	$10,000
Year 9	$20,000
Year 18	$40,000
Year 27	$80,000
Year 36	$160,000

Of course, that doesn't take into account that you will continue to contribute funds into the account annually, and returns aren't guaranteed. The example above is oversimplified, there's still a lot of math involved, but you should get the idea. When you place funds into a 401k savings plan, it will also reduce your taxable income. For example, to keep things simple, if you earn $60,000 a year and place $6000 in a 401k, your taxable income for the year will be $54,000, ignoring other pretax deductions, such as health insurance and social security. You'll be taxed at the time of withdrawal, which hopefully is way down the road. However, companies may provide different 401k vehicles for employees to invest in and the impact of taxes may be different for each person, so make sure to do plenty of research.

You'll most likely experience periods of growth and periods of negative returns. One year my 401k portfolio experienced a ridiculous rate of return, and it was negative on another. Keep in mind that a 401k is a long-term investment. Disclaimer: I'm not a finance professional, so do your homework or speak with a financial advisor to get started if you haven't already. Be sure to review the fund offerings and evaluate their historical performances before investing in them. There may be times where you may consider pulling the funds out of the account due to market volatility. If you do, know that there may be a penalty for early fund withdrawal. Happy investing!

Managing Your Manager

Most people hope for a manager like Michael Scott from *The Office*, but probably get stuck with somebody akin to Bill Lumbergh from *Office Space*. If you end up working for a large corporation, guess what, you're not working for the company. You are working for the manager. Unfortunately, if you end up with a crappy manager who doesn't have your best interests in mind, it may limit your career advancement.

We all know that management is primarily a top-down approach. However, that doesn't mean you have to take a manager for what he or she is, someone who tells you what to do. It's time you learn to manage up. It's time to manage your manager. I can easily say the best managers are the ones who gave me opportunities to lead and to develop my skills.

Learning to manage your manager is a foreign concept to many. Isn't management a one-way street? How does one manage the manager? What does it even mean? It doesn't mean telling your manager what to do because that would be a ticket out the front door with a foot up your behind.

It means helping your manager succeed so that you both can succeed. The end game is that if the manager is successful, so is the employee. Job satisfaction and management relations are interconnected. Remember, managers are not perfect, and they are people like you, despite what you may think of them.

Tell Your Manager About Your Career Goals. The person who is in charge of your career is you, but you cannot do it alone. Whether you prefer to stay at the current job level or to move on to a higher-level position, make sure to let your manager know how you want to develop your skills and which direction you want to take your career. Your manager isn't a mind reader That way you may take on challenging projects that will help you advance. For example, are you aspiring to become a manager? Ask your manager to be more involved in management activities and to attend management training classes. Doing so will give your manager an idea on how to manage your work. Think of it has helping your manager manage you.

Observe Your Manager. Spend time observing your manager, but not in a creepy kind of way, like following the person around and staring from a dark corner. Manager observation is a process that can take weeks, perhaps months. During meetings and discussions, pay particular attention to what your manager says and how he or she answers questions. The goal is to figure out your manager's management style. For example:
- Is your manager a micromanager that breathes behind your shoulder and nitpicks at everything you do? In this case, you better learn fast of what the manager is particular of. If not, it's not going to be a pleasant working environment.
- Is your manager more of a mentor who lets you work on your terms and provides job guidance to help you grow? It's a great situation to be in, just make sure to let your manager know what your career goals are.
- Is your manager the type to take all the credit for the work you do? This type of manager raises red flags and can keep you from advancing.
- Is your manager they type to empower employees with decision-making authority? If so, then your manager trusts you. Do your best not to lose that trust.
- Is your manager making you miserable? Start updating that resume.

Resolve Conflicts on Your Own First. Do your best to resolve conflicts or issues on your own before escalating the situation to your manager. Chances are, your manager will ask about what you did to solve a particular problem. Managers want to see if their employees can handle adversity on their own and should not be there to get them out of a jam every single time. We are all adults and are expected to take care of issues. Only escalate when necessary.

Complement Your Manager. Managers are not perfect. If he or she lacks a particular skill, fill in the gap if possible. Remember, if your manager looks good, you will look good. If you know the manager doesn't keep track of time well, give time reminders at meetings and such. If the manager is not a good presenter, help with the presentation preparations and rehearsals. If the manager isn't particularly organized, help bring some structure and order to the team.

Be a Mind Reader, Sort Of. Anticipate your manager's needs, expectations, and even questions. Be aware of your manager's behavior since we are creatures of habit. Certain scenarios or triggers may cause them to ask similar questions each time. Eventually, you'll be able to preempt them. Sometimes when I have one-on-one discussions with managers, I answer questions that they plan on asking. If you think like a manager, it will be noticed.

Provide Status Updates. Keep your manager updated on your progress. Weekly status reports are best for this. Chances are, your manager may report your successes up the chain of command, gaining you more visibility. In a large corporation, the more higher-ups know who you are, the better odds of you getting a promotion and a raise if they can see the value you're providing.

Realize that to be able to manage your manager you need to be in good standing with each other. If you would much rather feed your manager to a pack of hungry wolves, the situation obviously needs to be assessed. When you interview for a job, you will most likely be interviewed by the position's manager. It's as much of an interview for the manager as it's for you. You will have to get a sense of how well you two will get along. One of the questions I ask potential managers during an interview is about their management style. Since I have a particular work style, it's important that the manager can manage me in a way that doesn't disrupt my mojo, and also for me to get a sense if I can get along with that manager.

FROM THE CUBE FARM

The Conference Trap

Vendor booths and exhibitions at conferences are ideal for collecting free pens and stress balls. However, some vendors will raffle off a fancy new tablet computer or something expensive at the end of the conference. To get in on a piece of the action, the price of admission is a business card or filling out a piece of paper with your contact information. Without thinking much of it, I would unload my business cards into each vendor's raffle box, hoping to be the owner of a brand-new iPad or some digital toy. Well, I'm an idiot. I eventually realized that it's a brilliant marketing ploy by the vendors. You see, by the end of the conference, the vendor will have amassed hundreds, perhaps thousands of business cards. Not a bad way to expand the database of potential clients for just shelling out a few hundred bucks for a tablet to give away, right? They've gained access to an enormous network of companies and people, and all it cost them next to nothing to do so.

It may be fun to drop your business cards at every raffle you see, but what you're doing is giving vendors your direct contact information. Be aware that they will start to contact you via emails and phone calls to pitch their services, and before you know it, you have lots of companies soliciting for your business. Think long and hard before dropping in your business cards at conference vendor booths since it may cause some annoyance down the road.

Notes

1. http://www.npr.org/2015/07/21/421148128/zappos-a-workplace-where-no-one-and-everyone-is-the-boss
2. https://talent.works/blog/2017/10/19/youre-5x-more-likely-to-get-job-interview-if-you-apply-by-10am/
3. Not an actual walrus, just a man who looks like one.

AGENDA ITEM 5: PLEASING THE MEETING GODS

The meeting is a brain trust of individuals gathered in a room to share ideas, to get things done, and to make a difference. Well, if you lived in a perfect world that might happen. Instead, Bob is trying his best to stay awake. Jane is tapping away on her laptop on something that is entirely unrelated. Elizabeth is answering a mobile phone call, and there's the meeting organizer, with no agenda to keep the meeting on track. There are other people on the conference bridge, but they probably pressed the mute button and aren't paying attention. At the end of the meeting, nothing got accomplished, except for wasting everyone else's time.

Meetings are such a critical component of daily office life that I felt it deserved its own chapter. Many meetings fail due to poor planning and poor meeting management. If you can control the meeting, cover the items on the agenda, and everyone leaves with a sense of accomplishment, then you have pleased the meeting gods.

Chance Favors the Prepared Mind

Preparing for a meeting is not only about picking the time and sending out invitations. There are some things to consider. Why is the meeting required? What are you trying to accomplish? Who can give you the information you need? When are you going to hold it? Will it be an in-person meeting or a conference call?

Try to avoid scheduling meetings immediately after lunch hour. That's when food coma sets in. In a study conducted by YouCanBookMe, a maker of business scheduling applications, 2:30 PM on Tuesday seems to be the best time to schedule a meeting.[1] However, sometimes it feels like there's no best time to schedule one.

Location, Location, Location. When it comes to purchasing real estate, or looking for a place to start a business, a successful investment may come down to the location. While it may sound crazy to utilize this rule of thumb for planning meetings, it works. I hold and attend a lot of meetings. Through the years, I realized that the meeting location alone could have a significant impact on the outcome.

If I have to present a slideshow, I damn well have to make sure that the room has audio and visual capabilities. If I am expecting a large attendance, I better make sure the room has enough seats, and then some. When it comes to meetings with one or two people who have offices or large workspaces that have an extra chair or two available, I still prefer to meet with them in a different room. The reason? Why distractions of course. Without fail, a few minutes into the conversation, the person I'm meeting with suddenly receives a phone call, email, or an admin who just barges into the room to pass along a note. Those who understand the value of time give me their full attention and ignore such distractions. Occasionally, they'll pick up the phone and let the people on the other line know that they will receive a callback. But, there are those who genuinely test my patience. Sometimes, it goes like this: the phone rings and "Oh, excuse me, I have to take this, it'll only take a minute." Five minutes pass and I've already stared at every single piece of art hung on the walls, looked at the family pictures on the bookshelves, readjusted my posture a few times, checked an email, leveled up in the game on my phone, and getting ready to perform the cycle again. At this point, I want to leave. Eventually, the person hangs up, and there goes a piece of the limited meeting time. "Oh, I'm sorry, I didn't' think the call would last that long. Where were we?" "I was about to leave, and you wasted my time," is what I would like to say. The fewer distractions, the shorter the meeting, and who doesn't like short and efficient meetings?

PLEASING THE MEETING GODS ▪ 83

The Best Seat in the Meeting Room. Picture this, you arrive at the meeting early and face a long rectangular conference table that seats 12. There are many seating positions to consider. As the meeting chairperson, do you ever consider which seat is best for you?

Do you sit in the traditional power position (at either end of the table), near the corner, or middle? If the table is square or round, it doesn't matter as much on where you sit.

However, if the table is elongated, consider sitting as close to the center if possible. While the power position may be important, it isn't much of a factor for most meetings unless it's a board meeting and the CEO is in attendance. Also, if you're running the meeting, others will know that it's your meeting. Sitting at the end of the table will cause you to project your voice to the people sitting at the other end of the table. It's not an ideal position for soft speakers. Sitting at or near the center of the table will make it easier for you to speak and for others to hear you. Optimal seating position examples:

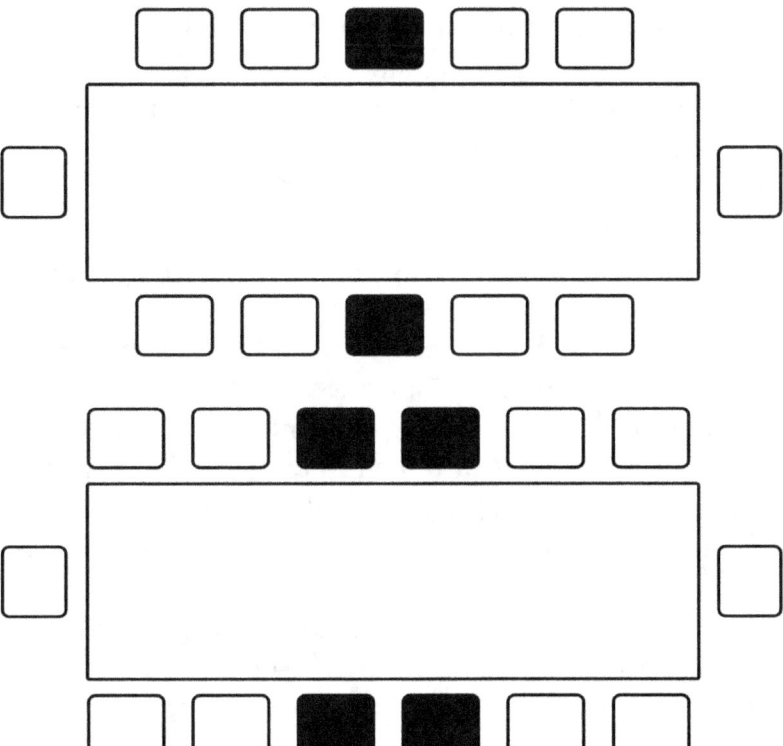

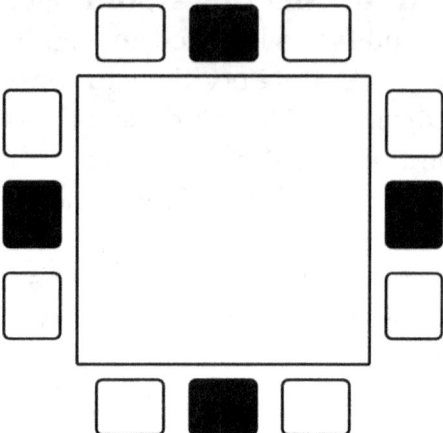

Lunch Time Meetings. Ever wonder how you can quickly become the most hated person in the office? Schedule a meeting during the lunch hour. There is usually one person who is notorious for doing this. Don't be that guy. Sometimes, planning a lunchtime meeting is unavoidable, and it stinks because it's the only hour your co-workers have to take a break from work. If there are no other options but to schedule a meeting during lunchtime, make it a brown bag session, or even better yet, feed the meeting attendees. It's hard for many people to turn down a free lunch. Also, try not to schedule meetings for Monday mornings since people need time to get settled, or late Friday afternoons since most people's brains have already checked out for the weekend.

People Are Forgetful Creatures, Use Reminders. If a meeting was set up a couple of weeks in advance, or longer, be sure to send a reminder a week before the meeting date and on the meeting day. Since we humans can be a forgetful bunch, there is no harm in reminding the invitees. Odds are, with busy schedules, some may have forgotten about it. Sending reminders doesn't make you annoying, just thorough.

The Agenda. The agenda is a powerful tool to keep a meeting on track. It's a meeting roadmap and surprisingly, seldom utilized. Invitations for meetings are sent out with the subject line filled out, but the body of the invitation usually has no details on what the meeting will cover.

There are no formal rules on how to create an agenda; but at the very least, present an outline of topics for the meeting, with a little bit of detail surrounding them. Detailed agendas list out the invitees, topics, duration of each topic, and the person speaking on each topic.

Send out the agenda at least 24 hours in advance of the meeting so that the invitees have time to review it. Sometimes, that is not possible due to spontaneous meetings that pop up but do your best in providing an agenda ahead of time.

Send out attachments with the agenda if possible. It'll give the invitees some time to go over the material so that they can provide feedback or ask questions during the meeting. It's highly recommended not to send the attachments right before the start of the meeting. Don't expect anyone to have time to review the attachments.

Consistent use of an agenda will show others how organized you are, and even if you're not, you can fake it well. It's simple to do and doesn't take much effort to create one.

It's Meeting Time

With the invitations sent, the agenda and attachments distributed ahead of time, then the one thing left to do is start the meeting.

A Quick Spot Check. It may be your meeting or someone else's. If you have been eating right before attending a meeting, stop by the washroom quickly and perform a quick spot check for bits of food stuck between your teeth. Keep a toothbrush and toothpaste at your desk. If any parts of your attire need repositioning, take care of that as well.

First In, Last out. Arrive on time to set an example. In fact, the meeting organizer should be the first to arrive and last to leave. If you need to use the projector or screen, getting there early to set it up may save time in case technical difficulties have to be sorted out. Book extra time if possible. For example, if the meeting starts at 2:00 PM, book the start time for 1:30 PM. If others are lingering afterward to discuss a different topic, it's fine to leave before they do.

Take Attendance. Take roll call and note down anyone who failed to attend the meeting.

Review the Agenda. Briefly, go over the agenda items. If other people are covering topics on the agenda, identify them in the room.

Take Notes. If you are a crummy note-taker, designate someone who is not. Recording devices are rarely seen at meetings but are useful for those who take poor notes.

Consider the Time Limit. Don't go over the allotted meeting time. Respect other people's time since they may have other obligations afterward. If using shared conference rooms, make sure to leave on time so that the next occupants may get their meeting started on time.

The Parking Lot. Sometimes, despite the use of an agenda, meetings tend to go off track due to the introduction of new topics or issues that come up. It's one of those things that tend to happen. The best way to address this during a meeting is to acknowledge them, and to place them in a "parking lot." Remember, you still have an agenda to go through. The parking lot is a virtual holding space for new topics and issues that come out during a meeting. Discuss those items after the meeting is over (or as some call it, "taking it offline"), or if there is extra time at the end of the meeting. It's important to place those new topics or issues on the agenda of the following meeting to make sure everyone is aware of the discussions that took place after the initial meeting.

Send Out Meeting Minutes. Before ending the meeting, quickly go over the follow-up items and thank everyone for attending. Send out meeting minutes within one business day. Give a brief recap and list the action items and next steps. It may not be possible to send them out immediately after a meeting due to other work priorities or other meetings that occur throughout the day. You are not always going to have perfect attendance, so the meeting minutes is another tool for you to summarize the meeting and to let others know about the next steps.

If there are after meeting follow-up items, list the tasks, owners, and the expected due dates. For example:

Task #	Task	Task Owner	Due Date	Status
1	Get cost of software from vendor	John S.	June 10	Open
2	Review requirements with IT	Jane B.	June 12	Closed

The Writing on the Whiteboard

The meeting presenter is having difficulty conveying a concept to the audience through words and decides to use the whiteboard to draw a visual aid, but you have no idea what it means because the shapes, arrows, and words look like a 3-year old drew them. Many people lack the skills to write well on a vertical surface such as a whiteboard or easel flip-chart. Heck, some people have problems with producing good penmanship because they spend most of their days typing and texting. When was the last time you sat down and wrote a long paragraph on paper with a pen or pencil? If so, did your penmanship look like crap?

People in teaching professions have excellent vertical surface writing skills from constant use of blackboards and whiteboards, but for the rest of us, we need to practice.

You may be in a situation that requires the use of a whiteboard or something similar to help get your idea or thoughts across to others. There are two types of whiteboarding skills. The first one is the ability to write neatly and legibly. The second is the ability to present your thoughts through words and shapes eloquently so that the audience can understand the information on the whiteboard. I've seen atrocities when a few shapes and arrows turned into a convoluted spider web of gibberish.

At the end of the meeting, remember to wipe off the board. There is nothing more annoying than going into a conference room and seeing "Do Not Erase!" on the board. The fastest and easiest way to preserve the diagram you drew or someone else drew is to take a picture of it with a smartphone. Make sure to delete it when you no longer need it for reference.

Have you ever found yourself in a situation where you have to write on a whiteboard during a meeting only to find out the marker is missing, or it's out of ink? You then excuse yourself out the room to find one. Or how about when the dry marker eraser is missing, and you end up wiping the board with your hands? Avoid these particular scenarios by bringing your dry-erase marker and eraser set.

Surviving Meetings

So, let's turn the tables around. Now you're attending someone else's meeting. Whether you're a major contributor at the meeting or there on someone's behalf, do your best to stay engaged.

Take Notes. It will help you focus and activate those two funny radar-dish looking things on each side of your head. Drawing spiral designs and squiggly lines don't qualify as note-taking. Use pen and paper to take notes instead of a laptop. The tapping of the keys is disruptive to others in the room, and especially to those who are listening in through the conference bridge.

Attend the Meeting in Person. With the option of dialing in or going to the meeting room, if you're in the building, get your butt out of the chair. Even if you're the only person there, it means a lot to the meeting chair.

Announce Yourself. If you're attending the meeting via a conference bridge, don't be a fly on the wall, always announce your presence, mute your line, and remember to unmute before speaking.

Managing Phone Calls. Set your phone to silent or vibrate mode. If someone calls your mobile phone during a meeting, decline, or quietly leave the room to answer it.

Fighting the Meeting Sleepies. If you feel that you're starting to fall asleep, don't fight it in the room, it will only get worse, and people will begin to notice your head bobs. Instead, quietly excuse yourself out of the meeting, take a quick walk or get a drink. Once the wave of sleepiness passes, return to the meeting. Ever been caught falling asleep in a meeting? I have, and my manager was in the room. That was not a good day.

Sending a Proxy. It's not possible to attend every meeting listed on the calendar. You may be away, double booked, or simply too busy with other priorities. If that is the case, try to find someone to fill in, but let the person know what to expect. Give a brief description of the subject of the meeting, your expectations, forward any of the provided documents, and have that person return with notes. If you're not able to send a representative, decline the meeting and provide an explanation, the other person will appreciate the small gesture. Don't forget to ask for meeting minutes.

Be Wary of the Hold Button. If you're on a conference call, and a call is incoming on the other line, don't place the conference call on hold because it may broadcast hold music into the line. If a call on the other line can't wait, leave the conference call and log back in after.

Rescheduling Meetings

The meeting has been set up, and all that's left is to hold it. However, the meeting gods are in a bad mood and the people supposed to be at the meeting have been pulled away into a last-minute client meeting. The clients will always be a priority, which means, sucks for you.

Stuff like this happens. There isn't much for you to do besides rescheduling the meeting. First, release the conference room reservation so that others may use it. Next, reschedule the meeting for a new date and time as soon as possible. Before sending the invite, remember to update the information in the invitation, such as the new meeting location or the date on the agenda. Fingers crossed that the meeting doesn't get rescheduled again.

International Meetings

In the buddy cop flick, *Rush Hour* starring Jackie Chan and Chris Tucker, both of their characters spoke English, but it was clear there was a language barrier between the two. When I was in Hong Kong for business, I used the word sneaker while conversing with a co-worker and he gave me a blank stare. When I said, "you know, shoes for running." He then said, "Oh, we call them runners!" Below are tips to keep mind when communicating with colleagues located in other parts of the world.

Use an Agenda and Distribute Meeting Minutes. Use an agenda to outline your meeting. Distribute meeting minutes soon after.

Be Aware of Language Proficiency. English is not the first language for most countries. Don't assume everyone is proficient.

Listen. Be patient when others speak and learn to be a listener. Just because you're more proficient in a particular language doesn't mean you should talk the most.

Speak Well. If you speak fast, slow down your pace, be concise, and annunciate the words. Avoid the use of slang. Don't try to force jokes, because they may come off as offensive.

Understand Time Zones. Be sensitive to everyone's time zones when scheduling international conference calls. Don't make them stay up late or get out of bed in the middle of the night to get on your call. You should be adjusting your schedule to accommodate theirs if you're setting up the meeting.

FROM THE CUBE FARM

What is This Meeting About?

A manager was not able to make it to an important meeting due to business travel, so she sent one of her direct reports, Mark to fill in. During roll call, Mark announced he was filling in for the manager. He then proceeded to say, "Well, I'm here, but I have no idea what this meeting is about or what I need to do. I'm just here because I was told to attend." He then made sheep sounds, "Baaah! Baaah!"

Online Screen Sharing Awareness

Virtual conference meetings are popular. Someone is usually sharing his or her screen through an online collaboration tool. Be aware that whenever you share a view of your computer screen online, others may be able to see the entire desktop. There are options only to show specific applications to online meeting attendees, but many just end up showing everything. On one occasion, a consultant was holding a web conference, and while she was waiting for other people to connect to the system, she was online browsing baby cribs and other non-work related sites.

Where Did Everyone Go?

I noticed a decline in in-person meeting attendance. Whether it was my meeting or someone else's, fewer and fewer people were showing up. Where did everyone go? Most people opted to dial into the meeting from their desks, even those who were just sitting a few feet from the conference room! Giving out a conference bridge number is a necessity at times, but only distribute it to the people who need it. The same applies to web conferences; many will take that option because it gives them the ability to multitask and not pay attention. It's frustrating when people dial into the meeting and don't respond when they are asked a question. Chances are, they are distracted. I'm extremely wary of giving out conference bridges unless it's necessary. I make a point that the conference bridge is for folks who are off-site, and I request invitees who are in the office be present in the meeting room. Another method I use is to only give the conference bridge number to those who are unable to attend the meeting in person.

Notes

1. http://qz.com/653033/heres-the-best-day-and-time-to-hold-a-meeting/

AGENDA ITEM 6: A PRESENTATION PRIMER

Believe it or not, your presentation roots go back, way back. For most of us, we had our first presentation experience during show and tell. Do you remember? You had to bring something from home to show off to classmates. Picture this: you're standing in front of the class holding something behind your back. The other kids in the class are staring at you. Look at them. They just want you to finish your turn so they can get up there and bask in the spotlight.

As your classmates' curiosity stirs, you bring out the precious object from behind your back and watch as they ooh and ahh in amazement. Timmy, on the other hand, is in the back row looking kind of worried and wondering why the frog stored in his shoebox hasn't moved in hours. It will be alright Timmy...Mr. Frog was very sleepy after a night of binge drinking with his friends. Whatever jitters you had before are now gone. Congratulations, you finished your first presentation!

If you were told to give a presentation on a random subject, would you be able to? Love them or hate them, the idea of giving a presentation tends to send chills down our spines. Nothing looks worse than watching an unprepared presenter struggle and not connect with the audience.

You may be thinking that you will never have to give a presentation in your career. However, experience tells us never to say never. As you climb the ranks and interact with more senior employees, you may have to give a presentation. Furthermore, if you decide to apply for more senior roles, you may be asked to give a presentation as part of the interview process. That's right, you don't even have the job yet, and there is already work to do.

While there is no guarantee that you will turn into a lean-mean presenting machine, there are simple things to help you get moving along and to make sure you don't end up like Timmy in the front room with a dead frog in the box.

Getting into a Presentation Frame of Mind

Ok, are you ready to present? Are you psyched? Let's do this! Smack your face a few times and scream at the top of your lungs! It's go time baby! It's paramount to get into a presentation frame of mind even before starting to write or type out the content. Consider the following questions to get started.

Why am I presenting? A simple, yet necessary question. Surely there is a reason.

What am I presenting? Think about the subject matter.

Who am I presenting to? Know the audience because the presentation content has to be on target and message. A presentation to a busy executive is going to be much different than to an entry-level analyst, or to an audience at a conference.

What's the story? This is the hard part. It's not easy to tell a story. Review the content and think of real-life examples or personal experiences that will help convey the message. If there is no story to tell, focus on the sequence and flow of the presentation.

Where am I presenting? The location and environment of the presentation are important because you will need the right tools and to have a good idea of how to design the slideshow, should you choose to use one. Giving a presentation in someone's office is much different than giving it in front of a crowd of hundreds in an auditorium. Take the dimensions of the room into account. If you're giving a presentation at a conference, look online to find some information on the venue, such as the seating configuration, capacity, and the dimensions of the room.

How long do I have to present? The amount of time you have to prepare the presentation may affect the quality of the presentation. Furthermore, it's important to know how much time you have to present. It will impact how you layout your presentation and slideshow. Learn to be flexible. What if, at the last minute, you have to cut down your 15-minute presentation to five minutes? What if you have to extend the presentation by fifteen minutes?

How am I presenting? Think about how to communicate the information and if a slideshow is required to give the audience additional detail. Do you need a projector or screen? Do you need a microphone? Do you need to wear pants for a video conference?

Practice: Lather, Rinse, and Repeat

Whether you're presenting to an audience of one or a thousand, always be prepared. However, not all presenters are great speakers. Don't worry. There is still hope. An excellent presenter who comes to mind is Steve Jobs, the co-founder of Apple. His ability to captivate the audience, deliver an on-point message, and use a slideshow to complement the presentation hasn't gone unnoticed. His method for being so compelling in front of an audience is no secret; he practiced and rehearsed his presentations meticulously.

The good news is, you most likely won't have to give a presentation like Steve Jobs, but it's nice to know that even he had to practice and rehearse to give a strong presentation. Don't worry about being perfect. You just have to be polished and know your material (at the very least, seem like you do).

Allow Myself to Present to Myself. It's come to the point where the presentation material is complete. Now it's time to practice speaking. Practicing in front of people, even to co-workers and friends, is still frightening. Instead, practice by yourself first. Close your eyes and...

- Visualize the audience.

- Visualize yourself speaking.
- Visualize the use of the slideshow.
- Visualize the room you're going to be in if you know in advance.

Start talking. Say something, say anything. Give a 30-second introduction about yourself and ease into the topic. Don't worry if the flow is not right, or if it's a bunch of word salad at the moment. Avoid giving the presentation in your head. You need to speak out loud because while it may sound great on the inside, it may come out differently when spoken. Don't fret too much since it's only practice and fine-tuning will be necessary. Stand in front of the mirror and observe your body language. Are you too stiff? Are you slouching? Are you fidgeting? Are you folding your arms? Are your hands in your pockets? Are you moving around too much? You don't want to appear uninterested, too stiff or too closed off. Remember, your body language speaks volumes.

Don't be surprised if the slideshow requires modifications after the practice runs. Eventually, you will start to feel more confident and comfortable, and most importantly, ready to practice in front of a small audience.

Get to Know Your Voice. The manner of how you speak and the tone of voice will have a profound effect on the audience. If you sound like you have low energy, the audience will perceive you as not having any interest in the subject matter. If you speak too fast, your message may not get through. If you sound like a robot, the audience may fall asleep. There are a few things to consider when it comes to speaking to an audience.

If you speak fast, try to slow down. People in the room need to be able to hear and understand your words. If you're a soft speaker, practice raising your voice. If there's an option to use a microphone, take it.

Introduce pauses between sentences for dramatic effect. Which of these sounds better? "I ran into a bear in the woods and it waved at me" or "I ran into a bear in the woods, [insert two-second pause] and it waved at me."

Modulate your voice. A presentation instructor taught me to imagine reading a bedtime story to a small child. However, you don't have to go to that extreme, just remember to mix in a bag of highs and lows.

An Unconventional Method of Practicing. A good presenter never memorizes the words to the presentation. Instead, it's about putting the concepts and ideas you understand into words for others. Think of it as a conversation with the audience. When you speak with other people, you speak as if there's no script to follow. One of the methods that I use to practice my speaking skills is to record myself talking about a particular subject matter. If you watch YouTube videos of people explaining things, teaching things, or reviewing products, many of them are not reading off a script, instead they are just talking to the camera as if it is an audience member. The same goes with other people who are video logging (vlogging) about themselves. They point the camera at themselves and just start talking.

Try this on for size. Find something you like around the house. It can be anything. Then record yourself giving a product review on the item you selected. If you're not sure where to start, try writing down a few keywords about the item to serve as speaking points. Next is the most cringing part, watching and listening to yourself on video. You're going to hate the way you sound, but I promise you, the more you listen to your voice, the more normal it will sound. Observe your own body language: Are you stiff? Perhaps a bit squirmy? Are you making eye contact with the camera? Are you fumbling words? Are you using too many filler words? Is there a particular filler word that stands out to you more than others?

Words such as 'um' and 'like' are known as fillers. Presenters tend to use filler words subconsciously. If the presenter is constantly throwing out filler words during the presentation, the audience may think the presenter is unprepared. I hated the idea of filming myself at first, but once I got used to my voice, I was surprised at the high number of filler words I was using. The best part of using this method to practice is that there is no audience. It's just you and yourself.

Practice with a Mock Audience. When you're ready, practice in a room with no distractions. Invite a co-worker or two to be your mock audience and have them observe your performance. Ask them to provide feedback regarding your speech flow, fillers, tone, body language, hand mannerisms, pauses, and quality of the presentation. The more you practice in front of others, the less nervous you will be.

Anticipate Questions. Presentations rarely end without taking questions from the audience. Be prepared for a show of hands and questions to follow. You can make the Q&A session easier by going through your practice presentations and think about what questions the audience may ask. Make a list of questions you think may be asked, but don't give each one a lengthy answer and memorize them. You don't want to look like giving canned responses.

Rehearse. There is a difference between practicing and rehearsing. Practicing is more casual than rehearsing. Whether it's in the shower, on the way to work, or during lunch break, it can be done almost anywhere. The rehearsal is as close to the real thing as it gets. It's a dry run of your presentation before giving the actual presentation. You may choose to rehearse wearing the same outfit that you plan on wearing the day of the presentation, and rehearse the presentation in the same room that it will be given in, using the same equipment. To place some context around it, think about how an orchestra prepares for a big performance. Individual musicians practice their musical pieces at home. They gather at the venue days before the show and rehearse as if they are performing the real thing, dressed in their formal attire. It may not be possible to carry out a full rehearsal at the actual venue but look for the opportunity to do so if possible. A good way to rehearse is to book a conference room at work, hook the computer to a projector, and perform a trial run from start to finish.

The Night Before. Conducting practice and rehearsal sessions may help to reduce anxiety, butterflies, and fear not only on the day of the presentation but also the night before. Pre-presentation jitters can keep you tossing and turning in bed. Restless sleep will have a negative impact on your performance. Drinking a few cups of coffee to stay alert and awake to compensate for lack of sleep may take you right over the edge. Usually, this happens to people who don't prepare for their presentations ahead of time or do it at the very last minute.

Fortunately, you're not one of those people. Imagine the shape you'd be in if you did not practice and rehearse beforehand.

The Final Countdown

The big day has finally arrived. A cocktail of nervousness and excitement fill your body, but that's normal. You have prepared for this moment! Consider the following tips to ensure the presentation goes as planned.

Look Good and Feel Good. It should go without saying, dress well and groom well. It's a real confidence booster.

Eat a Balanced Meal. Eat well, so avoid foods that make you jittery, lethargic, or give you the poops. If you are not a coffee drinker, it's not the day to start.

Anticipate Technical Difficulties. Set up the equipment early to make sure you can start on time and to fix any technical difficulties. Make sure all the equipment functions and there is not a raccoon in the corner chewing on the power cables.

Have Paper Copies Handy. For slideshows, have paper copies ready in case the projector, screen, or computer has issues. Technical difficulties seem to occur at the worst times. It may not be possible to distribute paper copies if there is a large audience, but if you're only giving a presentation to a small group, it's a good backup plan. Don't hand them out unless a technology issue occurs, since they should be focusing on you, not the paper.

Water is Your Friend. If the presentation is going to be a long one, have a glass or bottle of water handy to keep your mouth and throat moist. Refrain from taking large gulps, or consuming the entire bottle of water at once, just drink enough to keep your mouth hydrated.

Silence is Golden. Kindly ask your audience to silence their phones before the start of presentations. It's a common request these days.

Questions and Answers. Let the audience know if you're taking questions during the presentation, or after the presentation. It makes a difference depending on how you designed your presentation to flow.

Keep Track of Time. Have a timekeeper if you're afraid of going over time. Far too often, many presenters end up rushing through the last portion of their presentation or don't finish because time ran out. A timekeeper somewhere within the room can signal how much time is left. Microsoft PowerPoint has a timer function you can use as well.

Expect the Unexpected. There exists a law that states whatever can go wrong will go wrong. It's called Murphy's Law. The truth of the matter is, things happen, but it's up to you to keep cool. If a technical issue occurs, let your audience know, step away to get tech support, and continue where you left off after it clears.

Plug it In. If using a slideshow, plug the computer into a power outlet. The low battery alert can be somewhat embarrassing and sometimes the computer may shut down without warning. Having a fully-charged battery should prevent that from happening.

Remote On. Having a remote to change the slides is extremely helpful. It will eliminate the need to stay by the computer every time a slide change is required.

Backup, Just in Case. Always have a backup copy of the presentation slides stored in an external device, such as a flash drive. Some people save a copy in their email or the "cloud," but a flash drive is much better because it doesn't need an Internet connection for retrieval.

To Send Presentation Materials, or Not to Send? It's a better idea not to send the presentation materials to those who are offsite in advance. People who attend a virtual presentation will often go through all of the materials on their own before the presentation starts. It may place you at a disadvantage since you will not be able to control the flow of information during the presentation. Instead, share your screen with web conferencing software.

The Microphone. Unless you're great at projecting your voice in a large room, a microphone will be necessary to ensure everyone can hear you. Wireless microphones are great to use because it gives you mobility around the stage. Using a lavalier microphone will keep your hands free.

Other Presentation Considerations

Shared Presentations: If a presentation has multiple presenters, it's crucial that all parties involved work on planning and designing the presentation together. Everyone has to know which parts of the presentation they are covering and that the transition from one presenter to the next feels natural. The practice and rehearsal should be no different, but make sure to know where the handoff points are from one speaker to another, or else there will be some awkward silence and finger pointing on who speaks next. Failure to have a good flow between or amongst presenters can give the audience an impression that the presenters are unprepared.

Prevent on Screen Distractions. It's a far too familiar scene. Just when the presentation is going well, a pop-up window from an application has stuck its ugly face right in the middle of the slideshow!

Turn off all applications and programs that have pop-up notifications. That includes email notices, meeting reminders, instant message windows, software updates, and anti-virus scans. They are distracting and can easily mess up the flow of the presentation. I have seen the look of embarrassment on people's faces when their personal instant messages pop up during a presentation. One time a former co-worker was projecting her computer screen and an instant message came in from her colleague writing about how much she hated the company and stupid people.

Don't Wing a Presentation. If you're an, "I'll deal with what comes along my way" type of person, then I hope you're good at spewing BS or have the gift of gab. The difference between a presenter who has adequately prepared and a presenter who isn't is quite noticeable. It also reflects poorly on you as a presenter. Why should the audience sacrifice their time for you if you're not willing to sacrifice time on your part to prepare a presentation for them?

Don't Be a Slide Reader. Reading directly off a slide has got to be one of the biggest, if not, the worst presentation foul. Remember, the slides don't manage you. You are the master of the presentation domain. The slides should serve as visual aids or provide examples to elaborate upon. The audience is there to watch you speak, not to watch how well you can read. If you're going to read off the slide, just send out the slideshow file and don't bother giving a presentation. Reading off the slides will insult the audience and waste their time.

Presenters sometimes use notecards as an aid and glance down once in a while to make sure they cover all the speaking points. That's alright, but what isn't is writing too many notes on the cards that the presenter ends up reading from them, face down. The notes on the card should be simple and legible.

Slideshows

There is no doubt that a well-designed slideshow can make or break a presentation. Remember, the audience is not there for the slideshow, they are there for you. The slideshow is just one of many tools in your arsenal to support a presentation. Over-reliance on the slideshow may hinder your presentation.

Most presentations, even ones delivered by professionals, are supported by slideshows. Whether the slideshow contains data, pictures, or facts, the content has to integrate well with your speaking points.

There's no crime in spending a bit of time to dress up the slideshow with tasteful colors, transitions, and graphics. However, what may look great to you on screen may look absolutely like triceratops dung to the audience. Below are some guidelines that should help you get going.

Go Easy on the Animation Effects. They are distracting and tacky. Only use animation effects if necessary. Watching a slide title zoom in, spin around five times, and then zoom out is excessive.

Pick a Subtle Slide Transition. Be consistent when using slide transition animations. Stick to one straightforward and clean transition through the entire presentation.

Determine the Presentation Screen Ratio to Use. While computer monitors and television sets today utilize the widescreen 16:9 aspect ratio, the default slideshow aspect ratio is still 4:3. That means the screen real estate isn't properly utilized. However, there is an option to change the slideshow size to the 16:9 aspect ratio. The decision to make when creating a new slide show is on which aspect ratio to use, 16:9 or 4:3?. The answer depends on the situation. For example, if you know for a fact that your presentation will be displayed on an 80-inch flat screen display, then go with the widescreen option. There will be times when it's better to stay with the traditional format. For example, I was giving training presentations throughout the company and even though the meeting rooms and auditorium in the main office utilize large widescreen monitors, one of the satellite offices provided me a projector that looked like it was bought at a garage sale. The projection screen wasn't any better. It was a beaten white pull-down canvas that was more square than rectangular. To keep things simple, I kept the presentation at a 4:3 aspect ratio for all locations. An argument can be made to create the same slideshow in both aspect ratios, but in my opinion, it is a waste of productivity when it comes to managing and updating of what is essentially, two of the same files.

Use Pleasant Colors. A blue or green themed slide design may work to your advantage. Stick to a soft blue or a soft green accent, nothing too bright or bold. Word on the street is these colors are known to increase productivity, provoke discussion, and give the audience the warm fuzzies.

Don't Worry About the Slide Count. There is no magical number or rule of thumb for slide count. It will depend on how you deliver the content. It's better to spread the content out than trying to fit everything into a couple of slides.

Use the Trickle Method for Releasing Information. There are two benefits from using this method. For example, your slide has three main bullet points. Instead of displaying them all at once, show the first bullet item and speak on it, then release the next. This will help you pace the presentation. It will also prevent the audience from reading ahead on the slide, which will take attention away from you.

Use Fonts Consistently. Pick a font or two and stick with it. The font for slide titles can be different from those in the slide body.

Make It Print Friendly. The slide contents should be crisp and legible when they are printed out in black and white or color.

Make It Legible. Make sure the text and graphics are legible for those in the farthest row.

Use Contrast. Make sure the font color is also dark or bright enough to read on the screen. Sometimes projectors or monitors may wash out some of the lighter colors, making them hard to read and blend into the background. Ensure there is enough contrast between the text and the background.

Make It Color Blind Friendly. It may sound a bit extreme, but you will want to avoid text and graphics that may make it difficult for the color blind to see. In 2015, a football game between the Buffalo Bills and New York Jets confused red-green color blind viewers because one team was wearing all red uniforms, and the other all green. Some viewers were probably thinking, "Why is the team tackling their quarterback?"

Number the Slides. Slide numbers are useful for printouts or during a presentation when someone asks you to go back to a particular slide.

Go Easy on Text Length. Don't fill the page up with an essay as the text doesn't do the talking. The use of images that take up the entire slide with a few bullet points or words to help deliver a message seems to be a growing trend.

Fill up the White Space. If possible, fill up the white space evenly, so the slide doesn't look sparse.

Check with the Marketing Department. The company's marketing department may be able to provide slideshow templates and design guidelines since it's responsible for branding.

Bring Video Output Adapters. If you are planning on using your laptop to present the slideshow, make sure you have video output adaptors available. For example, what if the projector you need to connect to only provides a VGA connection and your laptop has a mini DisplayPort video output port? You can purchase an all-in-one adapter that covers VGA, HDMI, and DVI connections.

FROM THE CUBE FARM

Know Your Audience

One of the speakers was presenting on the subject of computer security. The speaker was a professor of quantum computing, and he spoke to us as if we were computer science Ph.D. candidates. The slides on the screen showed graphs and charts filled with scientific computer science jargon that made no sense to the business-oriented folks in the room. Unsurprisingly, more than half of the audience's heads were pointed down at their smartphones, and I had to leave the room because the topic of quantum computing makes me very sleepy.

My First Conference Presentation

A week before my first professional presentation at a conference, a good amount of time was spent practicing at home. I went online and found the hotel's event space floor plan and studied the various number of seating configurations.

I fine-tuned the presentation and slideshow during the practice sessions. Two days before the conference, I rehearsed in one of the conference rooms at work during lunchtime and at the end of the day. It was as close to the real thing as I could get. In addition to timing each run-through, I also rehearsed on different sides of the screen.

On the morning of the conference, all I did was glance over the slides for one final time. My presentation went off without a hitch, and the feedback was positive. I didn't feel that nervous, although my pits were sweatier than usual. In all, it was a great experience, and I was glad to have a successful conference presentation under my belt.

Party Pooper

I was at a small two-day conference and was scheduled to present on the second day. I was not particularly nervous the night before because I spent a bit of time practicing and rehearsing for the past week. I made some new acquaintances, and we hit it off during dinner. We were all kicking back with great food and drinks. It was a fun night, and a few people in the group wanted to do a bit more drinking at a bar elsewhere. They invited me to come along, and I had to decide to either go out and network with folks in my industry, or go back to the hotel room and get some sleep. I decided to return to the hotel room to relax for a bit, watched some television, and reviewed the talking points of my presentation for a final time. Yes, I was the party pooper of the group, but the presentation was the priority.

What to Wear?

It was three days before the conference. I spent most of the time leading up to it by practicing every day. Consumed with delivering a strong presentation, I didn't even think about what to wear at the conference. Then I realized that when I gave presentations at work, it was easy to figure out what to wear. If you're presenting to executives or high-level managers, it's a no-brainer decision to dress in a similar manner as they do, or, at least, go business professional. If you want to be part of the big boys and girls club, dress like you belong.

For the conference, however, I had no idea if I had to go business professional, business casual, or sweatpants casual. I emailed the conference coordinator, and she replied that it was business professional. Find out what the dress code for presenters is in advance to have time to get your business attire altered if required.

AGENDA ITEM 7: ERASING THE BROWSER HISTORY WON'T DO YOU ANY GOOD

When I started working in Corporate America, the Internet's potential for integrating our lives with mobile technology was yet to be realized. Social media was starting to make its footprint on society, and texting was atrociously difficult with a flip phone. The term smartphone was primarily associated with Blackberry devices. When Apple stepped into the smartphone game, everything changed. People today have evolved from texting and driving commuters into texting and walking hunchbacks. Is it really that difficult to look up from the screen while crossing the street? I even see cyclists texting and riding in the city, struggling to keep their bicycles in control.

Me, Myself, and My Selfies

Mobile computing and social media transformed the office landscape. Not too long ago, it was considered taboo to check personal email at work. Checking a status update, indulging in a bit of web surfing, reading few personal emails, and instant messaging with friends from time to time during work hours doesn't seem to be a big deal anymore. As long as it doesn't affect productivity or place intellectual property at risk, some employers simply don't care. Some people even leave their personal email screens up the entire day. However, being so connected with technology also means an increased risk of electronic data theft, increased computer usage monitoring, and even loss of employment due to a risky social media post. Technology may have evolved, but common sense hasn't. Use technology wisely, don't be an idiot as it can make or break your career.

Personal Email, Instant Messaging, and Surfing the Internet. Even though going online to do other things besides work may not be frowned upon these days, companies may block instant messaging programs and access to personal email websites. It's a safe assumption that the company has web content filtering to keep you from accessing inappropriate websites or those that may pose an information security risk. However, be careful of what you click on because a Not Safe For Work (NSFW) or malicious website may slip through the cracks. Most companies don't completely block access to the Internet because it's a moot point. If people want to check their personal email, social media updates, and NSFW websites, they will do so through their smartphones. There's no good way to prevent this unless the company bans all use of personal devices, which is highly unlikely.

If you spend your day surfing the Internet, people will inevitably notice, especially if you sit in a high traffic area where people pass by all day long. Back when I first started working, cubicle walls seemed to reach to the ceiling. Then the industry trend moved towards the low cubicle wall and open floor designs to foster "better" employee communication. It also means more prying eyes and much less privacy. It must have been good for privacy screen manufacturers when the workspace trend shifted to low-profile cubicles.

The Office's Worst Kept Secret, But Be Careful. I do it, you do it, and everyone else in the office does it. Surfing the Internet at work is the workplace's worst kept secret. However, you don't have to look paranoid doing it. Does the following scenario seem familiar?

You have been working for a while and in need of a short break. After all, you earned it. A quick Internet surfing session is just what the doctor ordered. A couple of minutes later, the sound of nearby footsteps catches your attention, and you quickly close the web browser, revealing the email or document that was behind it. You say to yourself, "That was a close call, I hope nobody saw me surfing the hats for cats website, I should get back to work."

By the time you flipped the screen back to whatever you were working on, it's already too late. The person who walked by probably noticed you browsing the Internet on something not work-related.

There seems to be an unspoken rule around the office that it's fine to surf the Internet as long as it doesn't interfere with work productivity. As with most things, use common sense. Don't visit inappropriate or shady websites, download files, open files from suspicious emails, and install unauthorized software. However, that doesn't mean you're not placing the company at risk. Sometimes viruses or malware will automatically download into the computer from legit websites without the user's knowledge, and they can wreak havoc. One form of malware called ransomware renames and encrypts files, preventing users from opening them. Unless contained early, the ransomware may spread from computer to computer and could stop the company from operating. Usually, the only way to fix the problem is to pay the ransom for a digital key to unlock the files or restore from a backup. With the monitoring tools in place today, information security professionals can pinpoint the user who inadvertently downloaded the virus, down to the computer name, time, and website visited. So, surf safely and be somewhat paranoid if you encounter something fishy online.

Remember, the work computer is not your personal computer, even though many of us are guilty of storing personal information on it. Also, be aware the company probably has monitoring software that tracks employee external website visits, so deleting the browser history is not going to be helpful in any case. If you think the private browsing mode is going to prevent others from finding out what shady websites you've been visiting, think again.

Remember, Big Brother is Watching. In this instance, Big Brother is a group of applications that are monitoring and logging your Internet surfing activity and behavior. That's right, even if you're surfing the Internet with no repercussions, that doesn't mean the websites you visit aren't monitored and logged. The most obvious way to tell if access permissions measures are in place is if a website you're trying to visit is blocked. Remember, what may be considered appropriate for home browsing, may not be for work. Reports for websites accessed from your computer, as well as applications you managed to install, can be generated. How detailed can the user activity reports get? Down to the name of the computer you used to access an inappropriate website, access attempts, and the time of access. Further more, if your computer catches a virus from inappropriate websites, that can be traced back to you too. One reason people get caught surfing inappropriate websites is when a person with a computer problem calls into the helpdesk for support, and the technician takes control of the computer to troubleshoot. They essentially have access to your entire computer and Internet browsing information. Sometimes, they find some inappropriate stuff. That is, if you're browsing inappropriate stuff. Other monitoring mechanisms may be in place such as keylogging software that logs your keystrokes, and data-loss prevention software that limits your ability to send or copy documents outside of the company's network. Companies place these measures in place not to protect employees, but themselves.

Professional Social Networking Websites. Professional networking websites such as LinkedIn have changed the dynamic of how people and companies interact with each other. Should you decide to join and build your professional profile online, don't be surprised to be contacted by recruiters or even directly by hiring managers from companies with employment opportunities.

Remember, the key word is professional. Carefully consider the type of status messages or pictures that you post; otherwise, anything that portrays you in a negative light will make others judge you for the worse. Look at it as making the first impression before making the first impression. Use a crisp and recent professional looking profile picture. It's also easy to create one. Groom up a bit, wear business attire and under good lighting, take a headshot, and crop if necessary, pants optional.

It's also a powerful tool to use during the job interview process. You may be able to find out whom you're interviewing with in advance. Search for those people who may have a profile on a professional social networking site and "get to know" your interviewer in advance.

Depending on your privacy settings, you may set it so that you will know who viewed your profile. However, it goes both ways. It may be easier to set your profile to anonymous to show that you're not nosy or creepy. Chances are, interested employers have already completed a search for you online, so it's only fair you do the same to even up the playing field.

However, there is a bit of a downside when using the professional networking sites. Many companies that are looking to sell their products and services may end up bombarding you with spam emails and unsolicited phone calls. The worst part is the spam because even if you don't show your email, it's sort of easy to guess what your work email is, which is probably, yourfirstname.yourlastname@yourcompanyname.com, or something similar.

Personal Social Networking Websites. On the other end of the social networking spectrum, are the personal sites such as Facebook, Twitter, Instagram, Snapchat, or whatever the next big thing people use to share every aspect of their lives. Some people tend to overshare and do stupid stuff, such as checking-in to their house, publicly displaying their home address. Whatever you post, don't post anything negative that associates with your job or employer. Venting work frustrations on social networks is normal, but some people take it to the extreme. It may be better not to mention anything online altogether. You'll never know who will be offended, and there may be repercussions that may lead to losing your job.

Some companies have social profile policies that prevent employees from listing their place of employment on such websites. They are afraid that if you do post something inappropriate, it will reflect negatively on the company whether the post is work-related or not. According to CareerBuilder's social media recruitment survey, 60 percent of employers use social networking sites to research job candidates[1]. Over 25 percent of employers also reprimanded or fired employees based on the social media findings. However, if your online social profile presents you in a positive light, it may work to your advantage.

Furthermore, be careful of coworkers you accept as a "friend" or allow as a "follower." Some people are nosey and like to dig into other people's lives. There are those who may act like your friend, but in reality, may have it out for you. They could very well use the pictures or statuses you posted against you or maybe share it with someone who doesn't like you. It's best to keep your personal life separate from your professional life if possible.

Social Network Induced Envy. It's common for co-workers to become "friends" on personal social networking sites. However, be wary of who you decide to connect with and don't be afraid to decline invitations to connect. Explain to the requester that you don't share your personal online profile with co-workers. I do it all the time. They will understand. By becoming social media "friends" with your co-workers, you have given them the ability and permission to visit your profile page and dig as far back as they want.

In some cases, being online "friends" doesn't fare well for many. I have noticed envy and negativity arise amongst co-workers from different departments who connected through social media sites. While some people at work seem to have a warm and friendly personality, they may be nosy about other people's lives. For example, take posting about a promotion you received at work. If your co-workers see that post, they may be congratulating you on the outside, but deep inside, it's probably more like, "Not fair, I work twice as hard, and I never get promoted." True, it's none of their business on what you post, but it may harbor resentment towards you. Those people are not your friends.

Another example that gets others riled up in the office would be posting pictures from an exotic business trip. Some of your co-workers may think, "What the heck, I never get to travel for business, that's not fair!"

Eventually, envy sets in for some people, and they start to gossip about others. That's how rumors start, and you know how people just love to spread gossip. If you're going to connect online with a co-worker, it's a better idea to connect through a professional networking site.

Email Expectations

Email has evolved from the greatest thing since sliced bread into stale croutons. While it's a "can't live with it, can't live without it" productivity tool, it's usually one of the company's most vital systems. The dependence on email as the primary office communication tool has caused people to forget about that weird looking thing on the desk with a number pad and a handset. I often hear others complain that people are not responding to their emails, and when asked if they picked up the phone to call the person instead, the answer is usually, "No, not yet, I was going to do that next." Sure they were.

Email Overkill. Email no longer guarantees immediate replies, and some go unanswered altogether. While the purpose of email has remained relatively unchanged, the nature of it certainly has. Gone are days of expecting people to reply to emails within an hour, let alone a day. Chances are, many people receive hundreds of emails a day and don't have the opportunity to sift through them until later, sometimes, much later. While unanswered emails queue up day after day, it's not surprising that some inadvertently go unread.

However, many companies have circumvented this through the use of interoffice instant messaging programs. There is an accepted norm that instant messaging doesn't have to be as formal as emails, and is just as good as contacting someone through a phone call, if not better.

The advantage of using instant messaging programs is that they show the status of employee availability at any given time. A green status indicator means the person is available for conversation. A red-light indicator means "I'm busy, leave me alone," and a yellow status indicator denotes inactivity, meaning the person is probably away from their computer or desk. Use instant messaging to your advantage if your company utilizes it.

Tone, the Missing Element. In the same manner of how social media has watered down human interaction each other, the prevalent use of email and interoffice instant messaging has removed somewhat of a personal touch. When it comes to communication through text and not voice, one critical component is missing, tone.

The way people read email and other text-based communications depend on the relationship between the sender and the receiver. That is why email messages have to be clear, concise, and unambiguous.

The same message can be interpreted differently based on the sender's relationship with each recipient. Sometimes, emails are misinterpreted because the recipient is having a bad day.

Update the Subject Line When Appropriate. As far as email fouls go, this is the one that is most annoying. Sometimes when people are having a discussion on an email thread and the focus shifts to another topic, the original subject of the email is not updated to reflect the new discussion topic. Is this usually an oversight, or laziness? Change the subject line so that the new topic isn't lost under the old subject if it has to be retrieved at a later time.

Email Attachments. Sending an attachment to someone through an email is all part of the day-to-day. However, there a few things to consider as it's never as simple as just attaching a file and sending it.

Keep the size of the attachment reasonable. Some companies limit the size of employee mailboxes, and if they become full, the recipient won't be able to receive or send an email. Find out if your company has a document sharing system so you can send recipients the link to the file.

If you want to share your family vacation photos and cat pictures with co-workers, don't use your work email to send them. Instead, upload them to one of the many free online photo album providers and send the link to that album.

Make sure the recipient can open the attached file. Sometimes the recipient may not have the same program installed to view the file. In regards to sending presentation slides, you may be able to save the presentation in a format that lets it open right to the slideshow full-screen mode. Perhaps the biggest offense happens when people send spreadsheets. The spreadsheet usually is opened up in a funky view, and you have to reset the view or navigate through it to find the information. You may have printed out the spreadsheet only to find out the rows and columns are printing out in fragments on multiple pages. Here are some common mistakes people make when sending spreadsheets.

- The spreadsheet opens up in a completely wrong row and column area.
- The spreadsheet is not formatted for printing.
- The spreadsheet opens up at a reduced view percentage. What is this, a spreadsheet for ants?
- Multiple spreadsheets in a workbook don't have the tabs labeled.
- The spreadsheet opens up in the page break view.

Be careful when sending work-related files outside of the company's network. For example, you may send a work file to your personal email address to continue working from home. However, you have just sent sensitive work information to the outside, and that may be a violation of the company's information security policies, which could lead to job termination. Companies with robust information security measures in place can monitor such actions.

Email Rage! Me Smash! Someone pisses you off in an email, and you want to retaliate with a scathing and nasty one of your own. In the heat of the moment, it seems to be the right thing to do. Don't let the rage do the typing. You aren't dumb enough to leave a paper trail, are you? Yell at them over the phone instead! Just kidding. If you're riled up, then it's not the best time to reply to the email. The worst-case scenario would be to send back a rage-induced retaliatory email that further escalates the issue, and once you realize what you did, it may be too late to unsend the message.

Instead, write the email, but don't send it. Make sure the *To:* section is not populated. Another option before replying would be to take some time away from the email and think about your response once you're calm. Don't retaliate with the same type of malice as the original email. If the recipient becomes defensive and unreasonable, it will make things worse. You are better off replying sincerely. Having the email reply reviewed by another set of eyes before sending is also helpful. Sometimes the tone of the email may be misconstrued so maybe a civilized phone call would be a better option.

Email Archiving. You may never know when you will have to look for an old email for reference or information on a particular matter. You may have to play historian and dig through those emails. That is if you did not delete them in the first place. Meeting acceptances, calendar invitations, and out-of-office replies are ok to delete unless you work in a role that requires the retention of those items. Archive the rest in the computer since most companies limit the size of the email inbox.

Typing in All Caps. DO YOU KNOW WHAT IT MEANS WHEN YOU TYPE IN ALL CAPS? It signifies yelling. Use with caution since "raising your voice" via email may be taken the wrong way. If you want to emphasize something to stand out in text form, don't use all caps; instead, use italics, underline, or change the text color.

To Reply All or Not to Reply All? That is the Question. The reply-all email function, while useful, is also an occasional nuisance. I'm sure we have experienced or heard stories of people intending to reply to one person but accidentally replied all instead. Usually, it's not an issue unless the content of the email is particularly scathing or mentions someone negatively. Then there is the reply-all email chain, the one that involves a group of people who keep replying-all to tell others not to reply-all.

The act now, think later approach doesn't work well with email replies. Before replying to any email, particularly those that contain a large number of recipients, assess whether or not it makes sense to reply-all, or if the email is not important, ignore it.

Only You Can Prevent Premature Emails. You are writing an important email and want to make sure it's perfect before sending. You click the save icon often in case the computer crashes. Then an unexplainable brain fart moment occurs and for some reason, you accidentally send the half-completed email.

As you frantically search for the 'Unsend' option, it's too late, and your message read. You quickly send an email explaining what happened, and you feel like a fool.

I think we've been in a similar situation at one time or another when we somehow inadvertently sent an unfinished email message. We've been trained to compose an email the same way as writing a traditional paper letter. The process of writing an email is straightforward and rather conventional. First, type in the recipient's email address. Then fill in the subject line. Type the message, and send it. But why follow conventional thinking?

Instead, mix it up a bit. Type the message and fill in the subject line first. Once you're satisfied with the message, review the contents, then populate the recipient email address field. It takes away the risk of sending a message out prematurely.

FROM THE CUBE FARM

Not Safe for Work

I had a conversation with a computer administrator who told me the story of someone at work who was caught surfing pornography. After the incident, his manager asked him to install a more robust web content filtering program to see if there were other individuals accessing porn. To his disbelief (and amazement), almost half of the employees in the office were regularly surfing pornography. Some even started watching pornography right after they logged into their computers in the morning. I guess coffee wasn't the only thing that's required to keep people stimulated during the day.

In this digital era where many companies have the tools to monitor their employees' Internet browsing habits, I am surprised people risk losing their jobs by visiting inappropriate websites. In the United Kingdom's Parliament, in a span of four months, there were 24,000 attempts to view online pornography[2]. At a former employer, someone was caught watching pornography. It triggered a human resources investigation, and the information security team started to go through his Internet access logs. Let's hope no one touched his keyboard.

Job Application Denied

There was a job opening in my department and many internal employees applied. Having worked with many people, the manager asked if I knew any of them and was familiar with their work. There was one candidate that I told the manager to take out of the running because every time I walked by his cube, he was surfing the Internet, on social media, and looking up NSFW material. The candidate took himself out of the running as soon as he applied.

Better Late Than Never

Even armed with a mobile smartphone that receives work emails, I'm not able to catch up with the number of emails that come in. When it comes to reading and replying to other people's emails, I'm probably just as bad as the rest of them. The worst part is, I even check emails after work hours and during the weekend, and it becomes a new normal.

There are so many emails that get sent out throughout the week, and once in awhile, I'll receive a reply from an email that I sent out weeks ago. The scary thing is, I forgot it was sent in the first place.

Notes:
1. http://www.careerbuilder.com/share/aboutus/pressreleasesdetail.aspx?id=pr945&sd=4/28/2016&ed=04/28/2016
2. https://www.mirror.co.uk/news/politics/more-24000-attempts-view-web-11814706

AGENDA ITEM 8: BEHAVIOR BEYOND OFFICE BORDERS

There may be occasions where you may not be engaging in office-related activities in the office. Whether it's spending time with coworkers at happy hour, attending a holiday party, networking at a conference, or meeting with clients over a business meal, you're the unofficial face of the company. If you offend someone or act like a fool, other people will not only question your character, but your employer's as well. "How could that company hire someone like that?" The Internet is full of accounts of people losing their jobs because they posted something offensive and the company caught wind of it. Thinking that your employer will back you up if you do something controversial or stupid is a dangerous assumption. The most effective method of damage control that companies do when an employee does something that doesn't align with its values is to immediately distance itself from the employee. However, with so much emphasis on making sure not to establish a negative online reputation, don't forget that you also have to behave in the physical world.

After Work Party Time

For reasons unknown, some people tend to throw proper office decorum out the window when they partake in external office functions. Be it at an after-work social gathering or a holiday party, some think they are free from the chains and shackles that bind them to their desks, they can let go of their inhibitions. When out with co-workers, present the same level of courtesy and professionalism as you do in the office. In short, don't be an idiot.

Happy Hour. There's no harm in hanging out with co-workers over drinks after work, is there? Many people see it as a time to complain about how much their job sucks. But it's also about winding down after a rough day or a rough week at work. For some, it's the only time to socialize with others outside of work. Whatever the reason is for gathering after work for drinks may be, remember not to overindulge. You are going to be seeing these people the next business day. Whether you're a college student who frequents the bar with friends often or a professional in Corporate America who is no stranger to happy hour with co-workers, there will always be peer pressure. Know your limit and know when to say no. One minute you're talking to someone, and suddenly a shot of tequila magically appears in your hand in preparation for a group shot. Who even bought the shot?

The Company Holiday Parties. Either company holiday parties could be a lot of fun, or it could be a reminder of the high school cafeteria days where each table represents a different click. The jocks and cheerleaders are sitting together, and the computer nerds are at another table trying to avoid eye contact with the jocks. But much has not changed since high school, has it? The Finance team is keeping to themselves, the IT team is in their little world, and other departments are doing their own thing. Instead of hanging around with people you already know, remember that it's a chance to meet new individuals in the company, to talk to those you haven't been in contact for a while, and perhaps, to squeeze in some face time with executives. Make the most of the holiday party for yourself and remember to consider the following:
- Dress well. Dressing up with a bit more flair and formality is fine.
- Know your limit on alcohol consumption.
- Be aware of your table manners.
- Use the party to your advantage to network with others. What are the chances all these people in the company will gather again

in the near future?
- The question of "What do you do?" is inevitable when meeting new people, but past that stage, talk about anything else besides work.
- Don't get touchy and feely with co-workers. Men and women are guilty of this, especially when they become dosed up with a bit of liquid courage.
- Some companies allow their employees to bring their significant others. The rules that apply to you also apply to them. Besides, you wouldn't want the person you bring along to embarrass you or cause a scene.

If you work with other companies and vendors, expect to be invited to their holiday parties as well. You still have to be on your best behavior even though it's not your company's holiday party. By attending, you are representing your employer and want to make sure to keeping doing business with the vendor once the party is over.

Have business cards on hand. There is no obligation to pass out cards to everyone you meet, but if there is someone that you would like to do business with one day, hand out your card. Chances are, the other person will have one as well. Sometimes when someone hands you a business card first, and you're not interested in doing business or keeping in touch later, say you don't have one.

The condensation that forms on the glass from cold drinks makes your hands moist and clammy. Most people will extend their right hand for a shake. Hold your drink with the left hand to avoid moist hand shaking awkwardness.

Expect to do a lot of handshaking to everyone you meet and giving an occasional hug to the opposite sex. Bring hand sanitizer if you're worried about germs or you could just wipe your hand on a colleague's shoulder.

Back in the day, the company I worked at held lavish holiday parties. On one occasion, the holiday party took place at the American Museum of Natural History in New York City. The entire building was rented out for the night. There is something magical about being in a museum after hours. People were drinking, eating, dancing, and having a great time. Some, I could tell, had a little bit too much to drink. When I first witnessed this, I thought, is it appropriate to let yourself go at a company function? I figure common sense would dictate oneself to have a bit more self-restraint. Then the recession hit and those parties were downsized to a holiday potluck in the company cafeteria. It was a sad premonition suggesting raises and bonuses for that year were going to suck as well.

At another holiday party for a different job, a couple of people were on a table dancing towards the end of the evening. Do you know what that's called? A potential lawsuit. Clearly intoxicated, clearly letting alcohol get the better of them, and clearly going to regret it the next day. Friends don't let friends dance on tables at company functions.

Cameras are Everywhere. I'm not referring to security cameras, but camera phones. People will either be taking pictures or shooting video at some point during business outings, and there's a high probability that those pictures and videos may end up on social media. With mobile phones being able to take pictures in high resolution and having the capability to record videos in ultra high definition (4K), sharing high-quality media with others over the Internet has never been easier and convenient. So the next time you're out and are thinking of doing something stupid, remember, there's bound to be someone with a camera ready to capture the moment.

Business Nom Noms

Let's talk about one of my favorite topics, food. I'm getting hungry already. Eating good food and talking business go hand and hand together, do they not? While at a fancy business dinner, the urge to order everything on the menu will be tempting, after all, someone or company will be footing the bill, not you. You must consider the restaurant as an upscale meeting room and not only do you have to be on your best behavior, but also show others you understand the basics of fine dining.

Know Your Alcohol. Business meals, especially dinners, may be accompanied by alcohol. Whether the meal is at a casual restaurant or someplace that requires you to wear fancy pants, it helps to know about the typical beer types and wine varieties. A quick Internet search should get you up to speed real fast. With enough research, you may be able to impress your colleagues a bit.

- Common Beer Types: Ale, Stout, Lager, Witbier
- Common Red Wine Varieties: Cabernet Sauvignon, Merlot, Chianti, Syrah, Pinot Noir
- Common White Wine Varieties: Chardonnay, Sauvignon Blanc, Pinot Grigio, Riesling
- Common After-Dinner Drinks: Dessert Wines, Whiskey, Bourbon, Cognac, Brandy

Stick to the Restaurants You Know. When choosing the restaurant for a business dinner, choose one that's tried and true. It's not the time to take a page out of the *Indiana Jones and the Temple of Doom* dinner scene. Making reservations will save you some embarrassment in case the restaurant has no seat availability. Select a backup restaurant and make reservations for it as well.

Brush Up on Table Manners. Lunch meetings and dinner outings with co-workers and vendors are quite common. Your table manners will be placed on notice. Don't be the person who chews with an open mouth, speaks with a mouth full of food spraying bits and pieces of prime rib everywhere, or looks at the plate setting not knowing which utensil to use. If you're dining with others in another country, read up on its dining etiquette.

Don't Order Everything on the Menu. While business meals may be a chance for you to order as much as you want from the menu, don't. Even though the company or someone else is paying for the meal, be modest and order only what you can eat. Meaning, don't order the most expensive item or the entire menu. It's not about the food, but about engaging in a bit of casual conversation with a bit of business talk over a pleasant dining environment. Also, avoid ordering food to-go. When you have made your selection, close the menu and set it down. It signals the server that you're ready to order.

Don't Be a Food Paparazzo. Once the food arrives, you may be tempted to whip out the smartphone and start snapping pictures. Let's be honest, you're not taking the photographs for yourself, but to make your online friends envious and to get as many likes as possible. Remember, you're at a business meal, not a food photography session. Imagine the annoyed faces of others at the table when they are about to start digging into the appetizers and have to "patiently" wait for you to take pictures from every possible angle. It's terrible manners to do so, even if you see someone else do it. If you must take photos of the food, go back to the restaurant on your own time, if possible.

Why Are There So Many Forks and Spoons? There may be times when a business dinner will be at a fine-dining establishment, a place you can only dream of dining at. As you sit down, you try not to look confused upon noticing the elaborate table settings. "Why are there two forks on the left side, do I hold one in each hand?" The typical table setting consists of a salad fork and dinner fork on the left side of the dinner plate, and a knife and spoon on the right side. A bread plate may complement the main plate. There will also be a water goblet and wine glass to complete the set.

The rule of thumb is to work from the outside towards the plate. The typical dinner usually starts with the complimentary bread. Nothing beats warm bread and quality butter in my opinion. The soup comes next, and then salad. When scooping up the soup, fill the spoon by dipping it into the inner edge of the bowl, moving towards the center. Next is the salad, appropriately paired with the salad fork. The dinner knife is for bread and butter if you haven't' already figured it out. The dinner fork is for the main course. Sometimes the dinner plate is for show and will be replaced by the main course served on a different plate. There are usually two glasses, one for water, and one for wine. Should you decide not to drink wine, the glass will be removed. Unfold the napkin across your lap. Don't tuck it in your collar. Sometimes, if you order a meat dish, a serrated knife will be placed on the right side of the plate before the main course arrives.

After the meal is over, it's time for dessert. Dessert is a funny thing. Either it can work out well with everyone ordering something, or it can go the other way entirely. Sometimes ordering dessert seems awkward. For example, I have attended many business dinners where everyone orders alcohol, appetizers, and a big main course, but when it comes to ordering dessert, we end up in a standoff waiting to see who pulls the trigger. Then someone says, "Nah, no thanks, I'm good," and everyone else follows suit. *Crap! I wanted dessert!* But I didn't want to be the first one to order, and certainly not be the only one to order when everyone else had already said no.

FROM THE CUBE FARM

The Steakhouse

The Managing Director took the team out for a holiday dinner at an upscale steakhouse. Everyone was excited for prime-grade steak and lots of wine. I, on the other hand, was a fine-dining ignoramus and did not buy into the hype. I thought to myself, "what the heck was prime-grade steak? Steak is good as long as it's not grade F, right?"

At the restaurant, everyone ordered either ribeye or filet mignon. Except me. The genius that I am, ordered the roast chicken. All heads turned towards me with a death stare. "How can you not order steak, you're at a steakhouse!" cried one my co-workers. I guess it was in poor taste to order chicken at a steakhouse. Of course, they made fun of me, saying that the chefs would have to go out and buy a chicken just for me, or the chicken was on the menu for formality reasons only. The following year, we went to another upscale steakhouse for the holiday dinner. This time, I ordered the fish. Just kidding, I ordered the ribeye.

AGENDA ITEM 9: A BUSINESS TRAVEL PRIMER

Seasoned business travelers know all too well that business trips can either be great, or downright miserable. Some love to travel, and some hate it. People who have never traveled on business may have preconceived notions that business trips are glamorous and exciting. Here's the reality of business travel, not everyone gets to fly first class, drink champagne, and arrive at the airport with a limousine driver waiting to take them to a client meeting. It's more like, waking up before the ass crack of dawn with crusty eyelids, hoping to make the first flight of the morning. Then you're cramped in economy class with other business travelers trying to make up lost hours of sleep. Shortly after landing, you're hailing a taxi trying to get to the client meeting on time. After the meeting, you're hoping to get to the airport in time to catch the flight back home. Don't assume all business travel involves flying on an airplane. Driving an hour to another office location or a meeting also qualifies as business travel. However, if you can travel to other countries and experience their culture on the company's dime, consider yourself lucky.

Travel Basics

Whether you're new or a seasoned business traveler, the more advanced preparation, the less stress and worry you'll have if plans go awry. Whether you're traveling domestic or international, consider the following.

Don't Have a False Sense of Security. It's recommended to do a bit of reconnaissance on the destination before arrival. A quick search on the Internet should be able to provide information on how safe the destination is. Read other people's comments and testimonials on which areas are safe to visit, and which areas to avoid. Get an idea of the type of crime that is committed most often. This advice is not to scare you away in any way, but it's important not to go somewhere with a false sense of security. A vigilant traveler is a smart traveler.

Try to in Mix Business and Pleasure. Mixing in a bit of pleasure during business trips, especially if it's someplace foreign or exotic, is always good if you end up someplace worth exploring and if time permits. It's recommended to plan for this in advance so that after you finish business for the day, you don't waste time planning out what to do and where to go. Plot out your route and places you want to visit.

Opt for Extra Leg Room. While business class is always the preferred choice when it comes to business air travel, sometimes it's not available, and it can be tough to do work without the usual creature comforts. Trying to perform work on a laptop in economy seating is challenging. There is barely enough space for the laptop screen to open all the way, and you're forced to type in a vertical fetal seating position. The good news is that many airlines offer premium economy seats with additional legroom for a modest price increase, but the extra space makes a big difference, especially if you're planning on spending a lot of time on the computer during the flight.

Know Your Food Budget. It's great that the company is giving you money to eat on business trips, it's supposed to. However, it doesn't mean you get to dine at three-star Michelin restaurants or order whatever is on the menu. You'll have a daily budget for food. Some companies are generous with food budgets, and some are well...cheap. Budget allowances may be tiered, for example, $20 for breakfast, $30 for lunch, $50 for dinner. Keep in mind the amount is also for you to cover tax and tip.

Manage Expenses. Save all your receipts for expenses. If the receipts are not in your native language, write in the back of what you ate, when, and where. It will make expense itemization much easier. After a co-worker returned from an Asia trip, she could not make heads from tails between her business trip receipts and personal receipts. If paying cash, remember to ask for a receipt or write down where you ate and how much.

Take Advantage of Reward Points. When it comes to business travel, all travelers need to take advantage of signing up for reward programs to accumulate points for staying in hotels, flying, and using credit cards.
- **Hotel Points.** It's often better to stay at the large hotel chains since many different brands fall under a parent corporation. Use the reward points to book free rooms for vacations.
- **Frequent Flyer Points.** If you spend a fair amount of time in the air, sign up for an airline's frequent flyer program. Not only can the points be redeemed for airfare, but many airlines have partnerships with other airlines and retail vendors that accept miles in exchange for items.
- **Credit Card Points.** Business trips are expensive. Lodging, transportation, and food expenses add up quickly. Most companies will provide employees with a corporate card to separate business expenses from personal expenses. However, one downside with a corporate card is that it doesn't accumulate reward points. Many people use their personal credit cards when traveling for business. The potential to accrue a lot of points is enormous. There is a caveat, depending on how long it takes the company to reimburse expenses; you may have to pay the credit card bill out of pocket for the time being.

Confirm Your Reservations. If another person books business travel on your behalf, make sure they get the dates right. On one occasion, I arrived in San Diego for a business trip and found out the administrative assistant booked the right days for the hotel, just not the right month. This advice goes for any other types of reservations that are booked on your behalf.

Keep the Passport Current. Make sure your passport is always up-to-date if, even if you don't plan on traveling overseas. You'll never know when it's needed. The renewal process may take a while if it's expired.

Packing Considerations

It doesn't matter whether you prefer to pack in advance, or last minute, just make sure not to leave things behind.

Know the Dimensions of Your Luggage. Checking in luggage and retrieving it later is an inconvenience. Usually, if your luggage is around the 22 x 9 x 14 dimensions, it will fit in the overhead compartment of US-based airlines. However, if it has wheels that stick out or has an expandable compartment, it may not fit. Furthermore, there may be agents in the airport security entrance line who may ask you to drop your luggage into the luggage measure. If it doesn't fit, they will ask you to check in the luggage.

Make Your Luggage Easy to Identify. To reduce the chances that someone may mistake your luggage for theirs at the baggage claim, tie something unique to one of the handles, such as a ribbon, bandana, or a piece of cloth from an old shirt.

Consider Rolling Over Folding. There are two types of packers. Those who pack ahead, and those who wait until the last minute. Whichever type you may be, roll your clothes instead of folding them. You will be able to pack more clothes in the same amount of space. You should also consider using travel compression bags that don't require a vacuum to suck the air out.

Pack Extra Clothes. Pack an extra set of clothes in your carry-on luggage. If you baggage-check all your clothes, and they don't arrive at the destination, there's no guarantee that you will ever see them again.

Like socks magically disappearing in the laundry, your luggage may end up in a mysterious black hole. If you have to purchase new clothes, find out what the airline's policy is for reimbursement. My friend arrived in Hong Kong without his luggage. He purchased an expensive suit out of spite, and the airline reimbursed it.

Test the Hotel Room Iron. Your wrinkled clothes may require ironing after unpacking. Make sure to test the iron on one of the bathroom towels to steam out any residue or impurities that have built up on the bottom of the iron. The person before you may have tried to make toast with it.

Bring Flip-Flops. If walking on the hotel room floor in socks or bare feet grosses you out, bring a pair of flip-flops for traveling purposes. The germaphobe inside will thank you.

Bring Power Adapter Converters. Universal converters work best because they will most likely work in airplanes and hotels. Airport stores sell adapters, but usually are more expensive. In case you don't have an adapter, the hotel may be able to provide one.

Bring Essential Medication. If you ever have to search for medicine for common ailments while in a foreign country, chances are, the labels may not be in your native language. The pharmaceutical brands you're familiar with also may not be sold in the country. While you don't have to be a traveling pharmacy, bring what you need or may need. Bring prescription medication and anything else that you may not able to purchase while away.

Don't Be a Cultural Ignoramus. If you have the opportunity to travel to a foreign country for a business meeting, not only is it exciting, but you also need to be familiar with the customs and cultural differences of the country.

Use Physical or Digital Phrasebooks. A pocket or digital phrasebook for the countries you visit will come in handy. Basics phrases and vocabulary are usually all you need to get around. Pointing and grunting at something will only take you so far. If you need help getting around, there are mobile apps that can translate foreign signs and spoken languages into your native tongue.

Respect the Local Lingo. Be aware of speaking to people who don't speak your primary language. What may be native to you may be a second language for other people. It's best to avoid street talk, slang, and anything that will confuse the locals.

Understand the Local Dining Etiquette. Understand the dining etiquette of the country you're traveling to. If the local people you're doing business with eat with their hands, so will you. If people are using chopsticks, don't ask for a fork. Learn about proper tipping etiquette for dining and services provided. The tipping percentage will vary, and tipping may not be required depending on the country.

Be On Your Best Behavior. Check with the company's travel department or website to see if there is information for employees on how to act in other countries. If the information is not available, then do your own research. In parts of the world where a handshake is perfectly acceptable upon first greeting, it may not be so in another. A thumbs up or an OK hand gesture may or may not you in deep trouble with the locals, depending on the country you visit.

Understand the International Dialing Codes. Make sure you know how to dial back home and locally.

Familiarize with Transportation. Familiarize yourself with the country's various methods of transportation and which ones are best for visitors. Car riding services such as Uber may also be available. Sometimes it may not be a good idea to get into a foreign taxicab.

Plan for Emergencies. Know the emergency services numbers for the countries you're traveling to. You will never know what may happen.

Register with the Local Embassy. Check to see if the country you're staying has an embassy. You may be able to sign up for emergency text alerts in case something happens in the country.

Make Sure Your Mobile Phone Works. Most mobile devices these days should have no problem working internationally, but international roaming is expensive. Check to see if your mobile carrier has an option that lets you use your minutes and data overseas for a daily fee. Some may even let you roam for free. Other options included purchasing a SIM card with rechargeable minutes at the destination country or renting a mobile phone before the trip. If you're not interested in the option of making phone calls, you may be able to rent a wireless Internet (MiFi) device from an airport to stay connected. If you have a company-issued mobile device, check to see if it can be used overseas.

Look Up Exchange Rates. Look up the currency exchange rate before leaving. While the company may be picking up the tab for business and travel expenses, there will be times when you get to explore on your own and will want to make sure you're getting the best bang for your buck. Look for a place that converts currency at a reasonable rate since airport locations usually, charge higher rates. Hotels often have the best currency exchange rates, but there may be daily exchange limits.

Bring Cash. Bring cash in local currency. There is no guarantee every place takes credit cards, especially local markets and small shops.

Activate Credit Card Travel Notices. Notify the credit card companies that you will be traveling abroad. Failure to notify them in advance may cause the cards to be declined because they may be flagged as stolen. Also, have a list of the customer support numbers handy. Should a card be denied or stolen, at the very least, there will be a number to call to have someone assist you.

FROM THE CUBE FARM

What Kind of Pill is This?

During one of my visits to Tokyo, I developed an excruciating stomach ache from overeating. A pharmacy was located a few blocks from the hotel. Inside, I was expecting to see familiar over the counter medications. Nothing looked familiar, and everything had Japanese labels. I managed to find the pharmacist and pulled out my phrasebook to indicate I had a stomachache. He went over to one of the aisles and selected a small box of stomach medication for me. Whatever he gave me did not ease the pain. The pills could have been gumballs for all I knew.

The Flight Delay

I was at the airport waiting for my return to the States from Tokyo. About an hour before departure, the status of my departing flight changed from on-time to delayed. As the hour passed, the departure time got worse, and eventually showed the flight was delayed for 22 hours. The delay was due to a drunk passenger in first class on the inbound flight before takeoff. He created such a scene that the plane had to turn back, causing the pilots and flight attendants to go over their maximum allotted work hours for the day. The flight had to depart the next day. At that point, I had to get a hotel for the night. That was not the problem. The problem was that I had checked my luggage. I should have packed an extra set of clothes in my carry-on bag. I purchased a fresh set of underwear, socks, and t-shirt from one of the local stores in the airport. There was no way I was going to wear the same set of soiled clothes from the day before, especially on an 11-hour flight.

The Consultant on the Plane

Sometimes I strike up a conversation with the person sitting next to me. One time I ended up talking to a consultant who hated traveling. He told me that he was burnt out from the commute. His company had sent him to work on a project in a small town. He lived in Los Angeles, and he was on his way to some small town in Indiana. His commute required two connections and an hour drive to the project site. Every

Monday he commuted to the tiny town and returned to Los Angeles either on Thursday or Friday. He said he had been doing it for a few months, and the travel had burnt him out within the first few weeks of the project. At least, he's racking up the miles, right?

All Bowed Out

I am fortunate to have had the opportunity to travel internationally for business. Out of all the places visited, Japan had the greatest impact. People greet each other in Japan by bowing. At times, I didn't even know if I was doing it properly. It would have been helpful to have known about bowing etiquette ahead of time. A deep bow carries a different meaning than a slightly angled one. In 2009, Former U.S. President Barack Obama drew up a bit of criticism for improperly bowing to the Japanese Emperor. A bow foul, as some would call it.

I bowed so much on the trip that after returning, I unknowingly bowed to my coworkers after conversations. They had a, "what the heck are you doing?" look on their faces. A coworker asked, "why are you bowing?" Embarrassed, I gave a slight bow and walked away.

AGENDA ITEM 10: IN SEARCH OF GREENER PASTURES

It's common for people to change jobs often, especially with the younger generations who don't expect to stay at a company for life. Boredom, lack of challenge, stagnation, little monetary compensation, and being unable to fit in, are some catalysts for thinking about changing positions or employers. Sometimes, the only way to grow one's career is to leave the company in search of a higher position or a more challenging one.

The grass is always greener on the other side we tell ourselves, but is it? If you can find a new job, you won't know how great or how bad it's going to be until you start working there. You may have trouble adapting to the position, working with the people, or may be a square peg trying to fit into a round hole.

Changing Employers? Things to Know Before You Go

Whether you're new to the workforce or a seasoned veteran, the notion of starting a new job is quite exciting, and you want to tell the world. For those of us who have or are planning to leave their current employer for another, there are a few things to keep in mind.

Short Timing the Right Way. Even though you landed a new gig elsewhere, there is still a laundry list of things to do before leaving. It's normal to have the "Case of the Mondays" every day until the last day of work. Try your best not to slack off during the final days of work. You want to finish strong and not leave your co-workers hanging if your work has to be transitioned.

- Submit a formal letter of resignation. It's customary to submit one to your immediate manager two weeks leading to your last day with the company. It's in bad taste if you don't give your employer any advanced notice. Keep the contents of the letter cordial. If your experience working at the company has not been the greatest, then keep it simple with your date of resignation and that you will work on a transition plan. It's not a letter for you to voice your criticisms of the company and other employees.
- Prepare a transition plan with your manager and whoever is going to be taking over your work.
- Read the fine print on bonus payouts. Depending on the company's bonus season, you may be forfeiting a bonus if you decide to leave before the payout date.
- Check to see when your medical benefits coverage stops. You may have to find something to fill in the gap between jobs.
- Find out if the company will pay you for unused vacation. If they don't, take time off before giving two weeks notice if possible.
- Since the IT department will take back the computer, remember to delete anything that is personal or not work related. Personal files include documents, pictures, videos, music, other downloaded applications, and website bookmarks. If you installed any non-work-related programs, remember to uninstall them. The same thing goes for a company-issued mobile device. Also, don't forget to purge the browsing history. Most importantly, don't delete any work-related files. In some cases, your manager may request access to your computer in order retrieve the data out of it.
- Start working on your goodbye email sooner than later. Surely as the days pass, the list of recipients will grow. Try not to do it last minute because you may miss notifying some people. Walking out the door and then remembering that you left someone out in the goodbye email is a bad feeling. It's better to Blind CC (BCC) your recipient list than to list out the addresses for everyone to see. If your goodbye list is large, be prepared for an onslaught of congratulatory emails asking you where you're going. You are

not obligated to tell people the name of the new employer, so you can provide generic information like, "I'm going to a financial firm..." and so on. Send out the email a week before you leave and on the last day, send out a short and sweet final farewell email. Provide your personal email or save email addresses if you wish to keep in touch with others.
- Clean up your workspace. It should be as spotless as the day you arrived. Make sure there are no personal items left behind in the drawers.
- Say goodbye to those who you have close working relationships in person, because it matters. Don't wait until your last day to do so because some may not be in the office. Who knows, some co-workers may even want to take you out to lunch before you leave.

Taking Work with You. You may be tempted to take work files to serve as reference and templates for the position at the new employer. Well, before you think about plugging in that memory stick to transfer files or email them to your personal email address, tread carefully. We now live in an age where companies are waging battles to keep sensitive and confidential data out of the hands of outsiders. Once you leave, you're an outsider. However, most people who don't work in information technology think that information security deals specifically with preventing external hackers trying to steal information. Employee data theft is a significant issue. If you left your job and managed to leave with company information, you have committed data theft. In all honesty, who is not tempted to leave with their work? The behavior of departing employees taking company data has not changed, but companies today invest heavily in data-loss prevention measures to stifle such behavior. It doesn't matter if the emails were under your name or that you created the work, it doesn't belong to you.

Depending on the nature of the business you work in, the sensitivity of the data you have access to may be detrimental to the company if it falls into the wrong hands. There probably are data-loss prevention measures in place to prevent you from taking data, such as disabling the use of USB ports and blocking access to third-party email providers such as Gmail and Yahoo, and online storage providers such as Dropbox, unless access is allowed. However, if there isn't a data-loss prevention program in place, there may be some monitoring measures used to identify computers that had data transferred to an external storage device. Just because you can copy files from the company computer doesn't mean the company doesn't know.

Burning Bridges. Depending on the relationship you have with co-workers and the company, you may be tempted to give everyone you know stiff, double-handed middle fingers and drop the mic as you walk out the door. It's not worth it, leave gracefully with your dignity intact. Keep your exit interview cordial and provide constructive feedback. Which means, don't bad mouth the people, department, or company. If you're unhappy about something, let the company know and how it should improve on it.

There are people, however, after having secured a position with a new employer, who seem to relish in the moment of telling people off and speaking their mind on the last day of the job. You know, those who go, "You can take this job and shove it! I never liked you, or you, or you! I'm so glad to be leaving this place!" Despite how horrible your current job is, never burn bridges because it may come back to haunt you. What you're doing is severing professional ties with people you have worked with in the past, and that's usually a bad idea because it's a small world.

Instead of going down the fiery path, work at maintaining the established professional relationships. Leave with a smile on your face even though you didn't like it there. Former co-workers are excellent networking opportunities and sources of job advice.

Wait, You're Back? Employees come and go. In most situations, employees leave for better opportunities and perform well. However, not everyone succeeds in a new job. But the grass is always greener on the other side, right? Not unless the other side is a lawn full of weeds and patchy brown spots. The thought of asking for your old job back because the new job is not working out is embarrassing. Usually, people return to a previous employer into a higher position after gaining experience elsewhere. Besides, the vacancy you left behind may have already been back-filled. However, some people do end up returning to the employer they just left, back in either the same position or something different. It's another reason not to burn bridges and to keep relationships open with your former employers.

Many reasons cause a person to return to the previous employer. The person may have had trouble fitting in with others, was not able to handle the new responsibilities or the job was not as described. While it's not ideal to ask for your old job back, people will understand.

You Have No Power Here!

Poor company performances, mergers and acquisitions, and reorganizations are external forces that employees don't have control over. However, the consequences can be either very dire or very positive should you experience one of these situations. You may lose your job, be unaffected, or benefit from it. Let's take a look at the not so good aspects of working corporate.

Cost-Cutting Measures. When the company announces that it has to cut costs over time, one thing is pretty apparent, that changes are coming. It's not a good time for the company, which means the same thing for the employees. Rumors of layoffs usually surface when management uses terms such as, cost-cutting, operating efficiency, or reorganization.

High priority projects no longer deemed as such are canceled. Office perks such as free snacks, drinks, and beer carts (yes, you read that right) are sacrificed as part of cost savings measures. Budgets for conferences and training sessions get cut. Business travel is reduced, forcing many to use web-conferencing instead. Bonus payouts become reduced or eliminated, and raises are frozen. It's hard to adjust to the change and the only thing that matters to you during that time is, will you still have a job?

The Dreaded 'R' Word: Reorganization. The word that we've all come to dread, reorganization, makes us uncomfortable, like having a wild ferret in your pants. As the word spreads around the office, it starts to gain sentience. There are many reasons for the change.

Sometimes it's for better, and sometimes, for worse. Either the impact of reorganization may open up new opportunities for the team to excel, or it may slow down the growth of the team. People become promoted or demoted, teams split up, and new management and rules come into play. It's a world of uncertainty and worry. We tend to become comfortable with familiar surroundings, but in reality, the only constant is change. Look at it this way; because of the unknown, the impact of reorganization can be positive, negative, or neither. If it doesn't work out, there are a few options, hang around to see what happens, look for opportunities in other departments, or start looking for employment elsewhere.

Remember when I mentioned that it's important to keep a positive image and to say hello to people you don't even work with because one day, you may be working together? Well, reorganizations are a perfect example of this. If people already know you and hear that you're a good person to work with, it's going to make your transition to another team or department much easier if it happens.

Your reputation precedes you. It could either go like this, "Oh jeez, this guy is joining our staff, I hear he spends the day surfing the web and keeps to himself." Or, it could go like, "I cannot wait until that person joins, I have heard many good things about him from other people."

I have been in positive reorganizations that have led to promotions, but also one that placed my team under a new organization and senior management. The previous senior manager was heavily engaged in the team's work. After the reorganization, the senior manager that our team moved under didn't even bother to meet with us, even four months after the team had moved over. I couldn't work in an environment that lacked leadership or guidance. I also knew that my hopes of promotion stalled after the reorganization. Before the reorganization, my manager, and the previous senior manager were planning on promoting me to a manager role. That went away after the reorganization. Left with two options, to either stay or leave. I chose the latter.

The Expendables. I'm not talking about the action-packed, testosterone-fueled, explosive movie that stars the action heroes of the 80s and 90s. I'm talking about, you, and everyone around you.

There exists an illusion that as long as someone is assigned to a long-term project, consistently receiving high-performance appraisals, or is the only subject matter expert for a particular task, that the job position is secure. Not true. Many variables can lead to job loss. Project cancellations, poor company performance, mergers and acquisitions, and a whole list of unknown triggers means that no one person's job is ever secure. Is the company going to go down the tubes if you leave? If your answer is no, then you're expendable. The company will learn to get by without you. Life finds a way.

Job security isn't about how well you can keep your position. It's about how good you are in securing a new job somewhere else should the need arises. It's about having the ability to stand out from the crowd. Your resume on the job market has to be the tastiest piece of lure in a sea of employers in search of their trophy catch. Be that trophy catch, so that your new employer may mount your ass to a $900 ergonomic office chair.

FROM THE CUBE FARM

It's A Small World After All

Jessica, Charlie, and Monica work in the same department at Company X. All three report to the manager, Dave. Charlie and Monica don't get along. One day, Charlie announces to the team that he got a job elsewhere. However, Charlie's last couple weeks with the company didn't end well. He reported Dave to the human resources department for being a crappy manager. Fast-forward a couple of days and Dave told Jessica and Monica not to speak with Charlie. It's because Charlie had threatened to take legal action against the company. Anything they said could be used towards the case. Relations ended poorly with Charlie.

After Charlie had left, things settled down, and the team went on with its business. About a year later, Jessica secured a job offer with Company Y and left on good terms. At Company Y, Jessica's teammate was Thomas. They spent almost a year working together until Thomas told Jessica that he accepted a more senior position at Company Z.

A few months pass, and Thomas needs to hire another person for his team at Company Z. He receives Charlie's resume in his inbox. Looking over the resume, he noticed that Charlie used to work at Company X. What a coincidence, Jessica used to work at Company X as well. Trying to get more information, Thomas calls Jessica and asks if she knew Charlie. Thomas learns that Jessica and Charlie used to be co-workers and hears about what happened at Company X. Even though Charlie burned his bridge with Company X, it's still affecting him years later.

Didn't You Retire…Yesterday?

Finally, after giving years of service to the company, Elaine was ready to retire. A farewell party was held on her last day at the company. Copious amounts of food were served, and goodbye hugs filled the room. Her speech touched everyone's hearts, and it was sad to see her go. The following week, Elaine was back at her desk. Other employers were just as confused as I was. Didn't she just retire? I went up to her and asked her about the retirement. She said, "yeah, I retired from the company, but I'm hanging on for while as a consultant."

Out of The Frying Pan and into The Fire

When the company I was working at suffered financial losses due to the subprime mortgage market crash, everything went from spend, spend, spend, to save, save, save. Gone were the lavish holiday parties, seemingly unlimited meal budgets, and the complimentary beer carts. Layoffs were happening. It was quite unsettling to hear about the people you have been working with were walked out the door by a security escort.

The writing was on the wall. It was time to change jobs. The timing felt right because I plateaued in my current position and needed to go somewhere else to gain more experience. I started looking for a job and received an offer in a matter of weeks. It was too good to be true.

Everything was going great at the new job. The management team was great, and there were other people around my age, so it was a smooth transition. A month into the new job, senior management sent an email about an acquisition deal. "Oh, who did we buy?" was my first thought. As I read on, the company was to be acquired by a much larger one. Alarms set off in my head. "Alert! Layoffs are coming! Alert! Layoffs are coming!" What did I get myself into?

PARTING NOTES

Here we are, at the end. I hope you can take away something positive from the book. Even though your career path may experience volatile moments, it's up to you to steer it in the right direction. Through the good times, the bad, and everything else in between, use the opportunities and lessons learned to keep growing.

You may not be spending the rest of your life in a fabric-lined box. In the future, you could be calling the shots from the corner office with a view, or leave the corporate world behind. Don't be surprised after working for a while that you may consider a career change. You never signed a contract that binds your life to an office lifestyle. Maybe you're sick of working for the 'man' and decide to start a business of your own. Perhaps you have saved enough money to turn your hobby into a full-time gig. Maybe you and the corporate world are not meant to be. I know people who left positions in finance, consulting, and marketing to pursue medical, entrepreneurial, and writing careers. One of my friends quit his job and traveled around the world for a year. Whatever the reason and wherever you end up, good luck on your journey and keep on learning.

ACKNOWLEDGEMENTS

This book is a personal project that I thought would never complete. I can't begin to tell you how much this book has evolved since the first draft. Thank you, Ken K. and Julie K. for teaching me the importance of consistency and typesetting. Thank you James T., your experience as an author and reminding me that reading is just as important as writing, is advice I will never forget. Thank you, Alan N., my friend who shares the passion for writing. I remember when we both started to write our books, bounced ideas off each other, with the shared goal of publishing a book. Here's to more to come. Thank you to my wife for being so patient and supportive of my writing.

Of course, I want to thank you, the reader. Thank you for purchasing this book and giving it a chance. I hope you were able to take away something positive from the book, something that can be used during your career. Your feedback is valuable to me, whether it be good, bad, or ugly. Please let me know of any typographical or grammatical errors. I've lost count of how many times I read the book to catch and fix mistakes, but at some point, you have to say, "I believe in it, it's ready, hopefully it doesn't suck."

- JJ Lee, jjleewrites@gmail.com

www.ingramcontent.com/pod-product-compliance
Lightning Source LLC
Chambersburg PA
CBHW071544220526
45469CB00003B/917